ESPECIALLY FOR

....

FROM

....

DATE

....

Published by Barbour Publishing, Inc., 1810 Barbour Drive, Uhrichsville, Ohio 44683, www.barbourbooks.com

Our mission is to inspire the world with the life-changing message of the Bible.

Member of the
Evangelical Christian
Publishers Association

Printed in China.

3-MINUTE PRAYERS

FOR MEN

BARBOUR
PUBLISHING

INTRODUCTION

Got three minutes?

You'll find just the wisdom you need in *3-Minute Prayers for Men*.

This practical, encouraging book packs a powerful dose of inspiration into three short minutes.

- Minute 1: scripture to meditate on
- Minute 2: a just-right-sized devotional prayer
- Minute 3: questions for further reflection

Each day's prayer meets you right where you are and is a great way for you to begin or end your day. Read on. . .and be blessed!

THE BLESSED LIFE

*Blessed is the man who walks not in the counsel
of the ungodly, nor stands in the path of sinners, nor sits
in the seat of the scornful; but his delight is in the law of
the LORD, and in His law he meditates day and night.*
PSALM 1:1–2 NKJV

Father of all blessings, every day I encounter ideas and philosophies that try to compete with You and Your written Word for my attention. At best, these things are worldly distractions; at worst, they directly contradict what You have said. Please help me to stay focused on the blessed promises, commandments, and encouragements in the Bible. Lord, make me hungrier every day for Your Word. Help me to make Bible reading and meditation as much a part of my day as eating, drinking, and breathing.

THINK ABOUT IT:

*How important is God's Word to you? How can you make
reading and meditating on scripture a part of your daily life?*

VALUABLE TRIALS

*Consider it pure joy, my brothers and sisters,
whenever you face trials of many kinds, because you
know that the testing of your faith produces perseverance.
Let perseverance finish its work so that you may be
mature and complete, not lacking anything.*

JAMES 1:2–4 NIV

Loving Father, when life throws difficulties my way, feeling joyful goes against everything inside me. But Your Word teaches me that You use all things for my good and Your glory—and that includes the rotten things that happen. Please make me humble, and give me the understanding of just how much tough times can help me grow into who You want me to be. When I feel like complaining, please remind me that there is great joy in the easy times. . .and even greater value in the difficulties.

--- **THINK ABOUT IT:** ---

*Are you prone to complaining or negative
thinking when you face difficulties? How does
God want you to approach life's trials?*

KNOWING THE TRUTH ABOUT YOURSELF

*Here is a trustworthy saying that deserves full acceptance:
Christ Jesus came into the world to save sinners—of whom
I am the worst. But for that very reason I was shown mercy
so that in me, the worst of sinners, Christ Jesus might display
his immense patience as an example for those who
would believe in him and receive eternal life.*

1 TIMOTHY 1:15–16 NIV

God of grace, I often hear that I need to think highly of myself, that a positive self-image is the key to a happy and successful life. But I know better. So do You. Help me always to remember that my true value is found in the fact that You loved me so much that Jesus came to earth and lived, died, and rose from the dead so that my many sins can be forgiven.

THINK ABOUT IT:

*How do you respond when you are told that you must
have a positive view of yourself? What does the
Bible say is the truth about you—and all men?*

DIVINE FORGETFULNESS

*"No longer will they teach their neighbor, or say
to one another, 'Know the LORD,' because they will all
know me, from the least of them to the greatest," declares
the LORD. "For I will forgive their wickedness and
will remember their sins no more."*

JEREMIAH 31:34 NIV

God of forgiveness, it's so hard for me to think of You as for-
getful. Yet You've promised that once I've confessed my sins
and received Your forgiveness, You no longer give thought to
my past. In fact, Jeremiah 31:34 assures me that You don't even
remember them. Lord, help me to forget my mistakes and put
my past behind me. I know You have. And who am I to hang on
to things You've already chosen to forget?

— THINK ABOUT IT: —

*Do you ever think of your past sins and wonder how
God can so completely forgive you? How does the Bible
say God views the sins He no longer holds against you?*

READY WITH AN ANSWER

But sanctify the Lord God in your hearts, and always be ready to give a defense to everyone who asks you a reason for the hope that is in you, with meekness and fear.

1 PETER 3:15 NKJV

Lord Jesus, I confess that I don't always make the best of every opportunity to tell other men about You. It's not that I'm ashamed of You, and it's not just that I'm shy. Sometimes I wonder if I can answer the tough questions a non-believing friend may throw my way. I want to overcome my reluctance, and I know the only way to do that is to understand You and Your message even better than I do now. Prepare me, Lord, because I don't want to miss out on even one opportunity to help bring someone into Your kingdom.

THINK ABOUT IT:

What keeps you from sharing your faith with others? How can you be better prepared when you talk with someone who needs Jesus?

THE OBJECT OF YOUR LOVE

Do not love the world or the things in the world. If anyone loves the world, the love of the Father is not in him. For all that is in the world—the lust of the flesh, the lust of the eyes, and the pride of life—is not of the Father but is of the world.

1 JOHN 2:15–16 NKJV

Father God, this world throws countless temptations and distractions at me every day. If I'm not fighting off the lure of blatantly sinful actions, I'm dodging things that, while not sinful in themselves, have the potential to take my focus off You. I know that's just part of being a man who lives in a fallen world. When I'm tempted to stray, bring me closer to You. I love You, Lord, and I never want anything this world offers to come between us.

THINK ABOUT IT:

What kinds of worldly distractions challenge you most? How can you keep those things in their proper place each day?

KILL 'EM WITH KINDNESS

Therefore "If your enemy is hungry, feed him; if he is thirsty, give him a drink; for in so doing you will heap coals of fire on his head." Do not be overcome by evil, but overcome evil with good.

ROMANS 12:20–21 NKJV

Lord, I've heard it said that the best way to deal with someone who is angry at me, or someone who just doesn't like me, is to "kill them with kindness"—meaning I should speak kind words or do nice deeds in an effort to ease those negative feelings. I know that showing kindness toward an antagonist won't literally kill that person. But it just might foster peace, and maybe even a friendship, between us. Who knows? It might even open the door to a conversation about You.

--- **THINK ABOUT IT:** ---

How do you respond to someone who is angry with you or who has made it no secret that he doesn't like you much? What acts of kindness can you to do win that person over?

ASK, SEEK, KNOCK

"Ask, and it will be given to you; seek, and you will find; knock, and it will be opened to you. For everyone who asks receives, and he who seeks finds, and to him who knocks it will be opened."
MATTHEW 7:7–8 NKJV

Generous God, it's hard for men to get it through their heads that Your Word teaches that You *want* to bless guys who love You and come to You with their requests. I love You, Lord, but sometimes I wonder if I should really keep coming to You until I receive what I know You want to give me. I humbly ask that You give me the confidence I need to approach You, hands outstretched to receive what I need.

THINK ABOUT IT:

What keeps you from persistently asking God for things you know He wants to give you? How can you overcome that barrier?

OUTWARDLY FOCUSED

Do nothing out of selfish ambition or vain conceit. Rather, in humility value others above yourselves, not looking to your own interests but each of you to the interests of the others.
Philippians 2:3–4 NIV

Heavenly Father, I confess to You that I can be a selfish man. Even when I do things that look like they're in service to You, I'm often serving myself. Humble me and change my heart so that everything I do comes from a desire to serve You first, others second, and myself last. Show me today specifically how I can be more outwardly focused. Give me opportunities to care for the interests and needs of others in my sphere of influence. And help me do that with an unselfish spirit, a heart clean of any selfish ambition.

THINK ABOUT IT:

What steps can you take to become an outwardly focused man? What can you do today to look out for the interests of someone you know?

FINDING STRENGTH IN. . . WEAKNESS?

But he said to me, "My grace is sufficient for you,
for my power is made perfect in weakness." Therefore
I will boast all the more gladly about my weaknesses,
so that Christ's power may rest on me.
2 CORINTHIANS 12:9 NIV

Mighty God, You know how we men think. You know that we esteem physical and mental strength above most everything, and You know that the last thing we want to admit to is weakness of any kind. But Your Word tells me that when I acknowledge my weaknesses, You have me right where You want me. You want to empower me to do great things for You, but You also want me to acknowledge that without You, I am not just weak—I'm powerless. So, Lord, I embrace the fact that without You, I can't do anything.

THINK ABOUT IT:

Why do you think God wants you to recognize your own
weaknesses? What are the benefits of that kind of honesty?

WHICH MASTER DO YOU SERVE?

"No one can serve two masters. Either you will hate the one and love the other, or you will be devoted to the one and despise the other. You cannot serve both God and money."
MATTHEW 6:24 NIV

Loving God, this world throws distractions at me daily—things that can turn into idols if I'm not careful. One of those distractions is money, which can be either a tool I use to serve You or an object of my affections. Lord, forgive me for putting money too high on my list of priorities. You know I need to earn money so I can care for my family, but help me to put money in its proper place. Remind me that it is simply a tool to help me do things You want me to do. . .but it cannot be my life's focus.

THINK ABOUT IT:

How important is material wealth to you? How can you keep money from taking God's place as your master here on earth?

FREE TO SERVE

You, my brothers and sisters, were called to be free. But do not use your freedom to indulge the flesh; rather, serve one another humbly in love. For the entire law is fulfilled in keeping this one command: "Love your neighbor as yourself."
GALATIANS 5:13–14 NIV

Thank You, Jesus, for coming to earth to live and die and rise from the dead so that I could be freed from the terrible prison of sin. Keep me from walking back into that kind of bondage. I want to use my freedom to serve You and other people—not out of some need to atone for my own wrongdoing but out of pure, humble, godly love. I'm free, so now I can move my focus away from myself and onto loving You and others. Thank You for freeing me.

--- THINK ABOUT IT: ---

What does "called to be free" mean to you? How can you use that freedom to serve others with a heart of love?

PROPERLY MOTIVATED

"Take heed that you do not do your charitable deeds before men, to be seen by them. Otherwise you have no reward from your Father in heaven. Therefore, when you do a charitable deed, do not sound a trumpet before you as the hypocrites do in the synagogues and in the streets, that they may have glory from men. Assuredly, I say to you, they have their reward."

MATTHEW 6:1–2 NKJV

Lord Jesus, I know it's possible for me to do the right things for the wrong reasons. During Your earthly ministry, You taught Your followers to make certain that they never performed their good deeds or acts of charity in a way that brought attention to themselves. Remind me often to check my own heart to make sure that as I do good for others, my thoughts are of You first and of the person who benefits second.

THINK ABOUT IT:

What motivates you to serve others? What is more important to you: the recognition of people or God's promises of rewards in heaven?

THE POWER OF WORDS

Let no corrupt word proceed out of your mouth,
but what is good for necessary edification,
that it may impart grace to the hearers.
EPHESIANS 4:29 NKJV

Loving heavenly Father, I confess that I'm not always careful with the words I speak. I sometimes say things I shouldn't, words that could hurt other people and damage their reputations. And I don't speak nearly enough words of encouragement and edification. I know that needs to change today. Lord, please check me when I'm about to say something I shouldn't. Not only that, please give me words that build up and encourage others. Help me to replace my negative, hurtful speech with words that bless, encourage, and challenge others. Let every word that comes out of my mouth be helpful.

———— THINK ABOUT IT: ————

Do you sometimes find it too easy to say things
you shouldn't? What steps can you take to make
sure you speak only loving, uplifting words?

CONFRONTATION

*But when Peter came to Antioch, I had to oppose
him to his face, for what he did was very wrong.*
GALATIANS 2:11 NLT

Gracious God, confronting a friend or brother in the Lord—even one who desperately needs it—is one of the toughest things You call a Christian man to do. It's probably safe to say that no one likes being confronted, and few enjoy doing the confronting. When I recognize that a friend or brother needs someone to step up and speak some words of correction, help me to first examine my own heart so I can know if *I* need to make any changes in my own attitudes and actions. Help me to choose my words carefully so that I don't come off as harsh or judgmental. Above all, may my motivation be one of pure love and genuine concern.

THINK ABOUT IT:

*Do you find it difficult to confront another person
when his attitude and actions don't reflect God's
standards? What does loving confrontation look like?*

WITHSTANDING TRIALS

*Blessed is the one who perseveres under trial because,
having stood the test, that person will receive the crown
of life that the Lord has promised to those who love him.*

JAMES 1:12 NIV

Lord Jesus, You never promised Your followers an easy life, only that You would always be with them—even after You returned to heaven. Your Word tells me that trials and temptations will be a part of this life, and my own experiences confirm that truth. I'm encouraged and strengthened when I read that You have a crown of life waiting for me because I've endured every trial this world throws my way. Thank You for strengthening and encouraging me today and every day so that I don't just endure but prosper and grow as I overcome the trials I face.

THINK ABOUT IT:

*What kinds of trials and temptations have you faced
in your life of faith? In what ways have you noticed
God's empowerment to overcome these things?*

BEING A PRAYER WARRIOR

Epaphras, who is one of you and a servant of Christ Jesus,
sends greetings. He is always wrestling in prayer for you,
that you may stand firm in all the will of God,
mature and fully assured.
COLOSSIANS 4:12 NIV

Father, Epaphras isn't one of the better-known men in the Bible. But what's important isn't how well he's known, but what he's known for. Epaphras was a prayer warrior, and Your written Word honors him for that. Lord, I know You look for men willing to spend time before You on behalf of others, and I want to be that kind of man. I want to be someone who says "I'll pray for you," and then follows through. More than that, though, I want You to see me as a man committed to coming to You every day in prayer for whatever You lay on my heart.

THINK ABOUT IT:

Why is it difficult for some men to consistently
devote themselves to prayer? What can
you do to step up your prayer life?

HEAVENLY PEACE

"Peace I leave with you; my peace I give you.
I do not give to you as the world gives. Do not let
your hearts be troubled and do not be afraid."
JOHN 14:27 NIV

Lord Jesus, sometimes it feels like my life is spinning out control. Pressures at work, anxiety about my family, and other major concerns overwhelm me. I need some peace of mind, and I need it today. Nothing this world has to offer, not even the caring words of my best friends, helps. But You promised me peace, the kind of peace only You can give. Lord, calm my heart and ease my mind today as I bring all my worries and lay them at Your feet. And once I bring them to You, give me the faith it takes to leave them there, and never pick them up again.

—————— THINK ABOUT IT: ——————

What are you worried about today? What keeps
you from giving that thing to God right now?

BUILDING UP THE BODY OF CHRIST

We urge you, brothers and sisters, admonish the unruly, encourage the fainthearted, help the weak, be patient with everyone. See that no one repays another with evil for evil, but always seek what is good for one another and for all people.
1 Thessalonians 5:14–15 nasb

Lord God, You've given me the ability (and the responsibility) to help others along in their life of faith in You. And the things You've given me to do in 1 Thessalonians 5 don't require me to have any special training or education—just a willingness to reach out to my brothers who need it. Give me the courage to challenge, encourage, and help out when it's needed. Above all, give me the patience I need to deal with people who are as imperfect as I am.

THINK ABOUT IT:

Are you willing to challenge and encourage others in their walk of faith? How can you demonstrate patience with your brothers in Jesus?

INTERNAL CONFLICT

*So I say, walk by the Spirit, and you will not gratify
the desires of the flesh. For the flesh desires what is
contrary to the Spirit, and the Spirit what is contrary
to the flesh. They are in conflict with each other,
so that you are not to do whatever you want.*
GALATIANS 5:16–17 NIV

God of power, I thank You for Your Holy Spirit, who teaches
me, encourages me, and empowers me as I battle with my own
fleshly desires. I have a war raging inside me, Lord, and when I
try to overcome temptation through my own human willpower,
I fail every time. But when I rely on Your Holy Spirit, I have victory over my sinful desires. Thank You for making a way for me
to live the way You want me to live.

THINK ABOUT IT:

*What does the Bible mean when it tells you to
"walk by the Spirit"? What "desires of the flesh"
do you need God's help to overcome today?*

KEEPING THE PEACE

Do not repay evil with evil or insult with insult. On the contrary, repay evil with blessing, because to this you were called so that you may inherit a blessing.

1 PETER 3:9 NIV

Merciful God, You know me well enough to realize it's not easy for me to hold my tongue and keep from retaliating when someone speaks ill of me. But I know You well enough that I understand that this is not how I should respond when someone does or says something to insult me. On my own, I can't bless someone who does me wrong. So make me more like Jesus, who endured horrific insults and abuse, but did nothing but *bless* those who truly deserved Your retribution.

THINK ABOUT IT:

How do you usually respond to insults and other unkind comments? What can you do to change your approach to these things?

KEEP YOUR COOL!

*So then, my beloved brethren, let every man be swift
to hear, slow to speak, slow to wrath; for the wrath
of man does not produce the righteousness of God.*
JAMES 1:19–20 NKJV

Father in heaven, I understand that anger itself isn't necessarily sinful, and I know that You call men to speak words of truth into a situation when they are needed. But I also know that if I'm not careful, I can easily become angry when I don't understand the whole story—and then say things I shouldn't. Please give me a listening ear. Help me to hold my tongue when I don't have anything positive to contribute. I know that my own anger doesn't produce the results You desire, so help me keep my emotions in check. I want to avoid sinful, damaging anger.

THINK ABOUT IT:

*In what situations is it good for you to feel anger?
When is it not good to become angry?*

UNDERSTANDING THE TIMES

From the sons of Issachar, men who understood the times, with knowledge of what Israel should do, their chiefs were two hundred; and all their kinsmen were at their command.

1 CHRONICLES 12:32 NASB

Sovereign God, some days I'm confused and more than a little bewildered. I look around and see a world that is drifting further and further away from You and Your standards. It seems like many of our churches are quickly coming to a point where they no longer honor You as they should and no longer preach and teach the truth of Your Word. I'm not even sure how I should pray about these things, let alone what I should do. Please give me wisdom and understanding so I can know how to respond.

───── THINK ABOUT IT: ─────

Where do you turn when you don't know what to do or how to pray about something? What does God tell you in His Word about how to gain understanding and wisdom?

AN AGREEMENT WITH YOUR EYES

"I made a covenant with my eyes not to look lustfully at a young woman."

JOB 31:1 NIV

My loving Father in heaven, in this world it's not easy to keep my eyes from seeing things that can cause impure thoughts. I could stop watching television and going to movies, and I could completely cut myself off from the internet, and I'd still be bombarded daily with sexual, sensual images. The only way I could completely avoid these things would be to lock myself in a room with no media access—or join a monastery. I don't think You want either of these options for me. But, like Job, I can start by making an agreement with You—and with my eyes—that I won't intentionally look at anything that could stir up sinful thoughts.

THINK ABOUT IT:

It's nearly impossible in this culture to completely avoid seeing images that lead to impure thoughts, so what steps can you take to lessen their impact?

SERVING ABOVE REPROACH

We want to avoid any criticism of the way we administer this liberal gift. For we are taking pains to do what is right, not only in the eyes of the Lord but also in the eyes of man.
2 CORINTHIANS 8:20-21 NIV

God of righteousness, You tell me in Your written Word that I am to conform my thinking and behavior to the standards You've set for me, not to the world's standards. At the same time, You want me to examine my own behavior and motives to be sure I never invite scorn or criticism over the things I do for You. Lord, You've warned me that the world will oppose me because I serve You. May I never do anything to make it easier for people to criticize.

THINK ABOUT IT:

How can you make sure that you never subject the things you do for God's kingdom to criticism and scorn? What does 2 Corinthians 8:20-21 tell you about the importance of integrity?

DOING GOOD FOR OTHERS

Let us not become weary in doing good, for at the proper time we will reap a harvest if we do not give up. Therefore, as we have opportunity, let us do good to all people, especially to those who belong to the family of believers.

GALATIANS 6:9–10 NIV

Compassionate God, You've done so much good for me, starting with bringing me into Your family of believers. You love every member of Your family, and You call us to love one another in word and in deed. Lord, I confess that giving of myself to others, especially those in my spiritual family, can sometimes be draining. Please fill my heart with a desire to selflessly serve others, then give me opportunities to do just that. I love You and want to honor You by taking advantage of every opportunity to serve.

THINK ABOUT IT:

What can you do today to serve others, especially other Christians? How do you keep service to others from becoming a draining experience?

GIVING OF WHAT YOU HAVE

[Jesus] also saw a poor widow put in two very small copper coins. "Truly I tell you," he said, "this poor widow has put in more than all the others. All these people gave their gifts out of their wealth; but she out of her poverty put in all she had to live on."

LUKE 21:2–4 NIV

Father in heaven, I know You want me to be a generous man. But sometimes, because my bank account is so depleted, I find myself afraid to give to Your work here on earth. I confess that my fear often comes from not fully trusting You to care for me when I give from what You've given me. So make me courageous and faithful to give of what I have, knowing that it blesses others—and leads to blessings for me and my family.

THINK ABOUT IT:

Do you fully trust God to meet your family's physical needs? If so, how should that affect your giving?

GUARD YOUR HEART

"But take heed to yourselves, lest your hearts be weighed down with carousing, drunkenness, and cares of this life, and that Day come on you unexpectedly."

LUKE 21:34 NKJV

Gracious Father, many things in this world have the potential to weigh down my heart and cause me to stray from You. If it's not the daily temptations to sin, it's the legitimate cares and concerns that life on earth presents. I know You want me to follow You and serve You with an undivided heart—and that's what I want too. You've saved me and made me a part of Your family, so help me to show my gratitude by fervently guarding the new heart You've placed within me. Keep me focused on You first, and help me to handle the things that could come between us.

THINK ABOUT IT:

What kinds of things can distract you from following God with your whole heart? How can you overcome those things?

A MATTER OF TRUST

"Therefore I say to you, do not worry about your life, what you will eat or what you will drink; nor about your body, what you will put on. . . . Look at the birds of the air, for they neither sow nor reap nor gather into barns; yet your heavenly Father feeds them. Are you not of more value than they?"

MATTHEW 6:25–26 NKJV

My Father and Provider, I confess that I often worry about how I'm going to care for myself and my family. How will I be able to pay for the things we'll need in the future? Lord, please forgive me for my lack of trust in You. You care about our needs even more than I do. You have promised to provide for us, so help me to rest in the fact that You always keep Your promises.

— THINK ABOUT IT: —

What worries keep you awake at night? Why is it hard for you just to rest and let God take care of those things?

CONTROLLING YOUR TONGUE

*Those who consider themselves religious and yet
do not keep a tight rein on their tongues deceive
themselves, and their religion is worthless.*

JAMES 1:26 NIV

Lord God, I sometimes cringe when I read James 1:26. I confess that I occasionally say things that I know don't please You—things that don't encourage or build up others. On my own, it seems that I can't control my tongue any more than I can keep my mind pure or my actions blameless. Forgive me for saying things I shouldn't. Help me to speak only words that glorify You and benefit my brothers and sisters in Christ. And when I don't have something good to say, Father, please give me Your good words!

— THINK ABOUT IT: —

*Do you ever say things that displease God and
hurt other people? How can you change that?*

REMEMBERING

Then I thought, "To this I will appeal: the years when the Most High stretched out his right hand. I will remember the deeds of the LORD; yes, I will remember your miracles of long ago."

PSALM 77:10–11 NIV

Mighty God, You've done so many great things—even miraculous things—for me since I came to know You. I recognize that You want me to remember those things and to share them with others so that they too can see Your compassion and greatness. Thank You for giving me examples of Your amazing deeds—both in the lives of people in Your Word and in my own life and the lives of those close to me. Remind me of these things every day, especially when You give me an opportunity to talk to others about You.

--- THINK ABOUT IT: ---

Do you ever think back on the many incredible things God has done for you in the past? What are the benefits of doing so?

YOU CAN'T TAKE IT WITH YOU

Don't wear yourself out trying to get rich; restrain yourself!
Riches disappear in the blink of an eye; wealth sprouts
wings and flies off into the wild blue yonder.
PROVERBS 23:4–5 MSG

Father God, Your Word warns me over and over that I am not to love money or possessions, that I am to see them simply as a tool to serve You and other people. Yet the lure of worldly riches sometimes still clamors for my attention. Lord, forgive me if even the smallest part of me loves money. Remind me daily that my money and things won't follow me into eternity. Help me to trust You in my work life and finances, and help me to glorify You through them in every way.

THINK ABOUT IT:

Do you see money as something to accumulate for
yourself, or as a means to serve and glorify God?
How can you best serve the Lord with your money?

GOD AS MY SHEPHERD

*The LORD is my shepherd; I shall not want. He makes
me to lie down in green pastures; He leads me beside
the still waters. He restores my soul; He leads me in
the paths of righteousness for His name's sake.*
PSALM 23:1–3 NKJV

Protector God, thank You for being a shepherd to me. A good
shepherd protects and provides for his sheep and guides them
to the best places to eat and rest. Then they can have the energy
it takes to do the things sheep do every day. But You aren't
just a *good* shepherd, You are the *perfect* shepherd. Lord, You
provide me all I need each day, starting with Your love and protection. You restore me when I feel worn down, and You would
never lead me anywhere but to a place of righteousness. Thank
You, not just for what You do for me, but also for who You are.

THINK ABOUT IT:

*In what ways can you see God protecting
you and providing for you every day?*

IT'S WHAT'S IN THE HEART

*"You have heard that it was said to those of old,
'You shall not commit adultery.' But I say to you
that whoever looks at a woman to lust for her has
already committed adultery with her in his heart."*
MATTHEW 5:27–28 NKJV

God of holiness, I can find myself falling into the trap of thinking that it's okay to consider sexual sin as long as I don't commit "the act." But You've warned me that allowing my heart and mind to go where I know my body shouldn't is as bad in Your eyes as actually doing the deed. Lord, it's so hard to control my thoughts. But I know that with Your help, I can do anything. Please train my mind to dwell on You and not on things I know displease You.

THINK ABOUT IT:

How important is it to God that you keep your mind from dwelling on sexual sin? How do you handle it when impure thoughts make their way into your head?

A PART TO PLAY

And He gave some as apostles, some as prophets,
some as evangelists, some as pastors and teachers,
for the equipping of the saints for the work of ministry,
for the building up of the body of Christ.
EPHESIANS 4:11–12 NASB

Lord Jesus, You didn't save me so I could go to church and just sit there every Sunday, doing nothing of benefit to my brothers and sisters in faith. You've given me gifts and abilities so I can serve, so I can make a difference in my congregation and in the world around me. Here I am, Lord. I want to be an instrument in Your hand. Move me and enable me to serve in the way that benefits others and glorifies You.

THINK ABOUT IT:

In what way or ways do you think God wants
you to serve at your church? What steps can
you begin taking to enable you to serve?

CHOOSING YOUR THOUGHTS

Finally, brothers and sisters, whatever is true, whatever is noble, whatever is right, whatever is pure, whatever is lovely, whatever is admirable—if anything is excellent or praiseworthy—think about such things.

PHILIPPIANS 4:8 NIV

Father in heaven, it often feels like my thoughts are out of control, like I am powerless against my worries, my lusts, and my pride. But You call me to think about much better things. I'm grateful that You don't call me to do anything that You don't empower me to do. You've given me Your written Word to shape my thoughts and Your Holy Spirit to control them. Thank You for giving me better things to consider when my mind goes places that don't help me or glorify You. Thank You for giving me the ability to focus on higher things.

THINK ABOUT IT:

What kinds of thoughts trouble your mind most often? How can you focus your thinking on what is true, noble, right, pure, lovely, and admirable?

GIVING CHEERFULLY

*Each of you should give what you have decided
in your heart to give, not reluctantly or under
compulsion, for God loves a cheerful giver.*
2 CORINTHIANS 9:7 NIV

Father in heaven, I confess that when I give to causes that expand Your kingdom and benefit others, I'm not always as happy as I should be. Sometimes I'm thinking I might need those funds to care for my own way of life. But Lord, You want me to give cheerfully, not with a worried or grudging heart. When I consider what or how much to give, remind me that giving toward the work of Your kingdom isn't just a duty but a privilege. And help me to remember Your promise to care for my own needs when I give generously.

THINK ABOUT IT:

*Do you think of giving as a duty or as a privilege?
How can you adopt a cheerful attitude when you give?*

A "NEW" COMMAND

"A new command I give you: Love one another. As I have loved you, so you must love one another. By this everyone will know that you are my disciples, if you love one another."
JOHN 13:34–35 NIV

Lord Jesus, during Your earthly ministry, You provided Your followers glimpses of the loving nature of Your heavenly Father—and You taught them the vital importance of loving one another. When You say that Your followers must love one another "as I have loved You," it shows me that You want me to love my spiritual brothers and sisters sacrificially, selflessly, and compassionately. Lord, You never intended Your followers to live self-focused lives, but that is just what I often do. Forgive me, and show me each day how I can love others the way You love me.

THINK ABOUT IT:

What are some practical things you can do to demonstrate Christ's love to others today?

SEASONING SALT

Walk in wisdom toward those who are outside, redeeming the time. Let your speech always be with grace, seasoned with salt, that you may know how you ought to answer each one.
COLOSSIANS 4:5–6 NKJV

Lord and Savior, I'm so grateful that You've forgiven me, saved me, and made me a part of Your family of believers. Your Word tells me that I am always to be prepared to share Your message of salvation with people in my sphere of influence. But I have to admit that I don't always know what to say or how to say it. Colossians 4:5–6 suggests that I should tell Your truth in a way that best connects with those I know need You. May my speech reflect my passion and love for Your message. And please remind me daily why Your Gospel is such an amazing message.

THINK ABOUT IT:

How can you best present the Gospel of Christ in a way that makes it appealing to non-believers without compromising the truth of the message?

BEARING FRUIT

But the fruit of the Spirit is love, joy, peace,
longsuffering, kindness, goodness, faithfulness,
gentleness, self-control. Against such there is no law.
GALATIANS 5:22–23 NKJV

Father in heaven, You call me as a Christian man to live life with certain character qualities. I confess that I fall short in many of those areas. I'm not always as loving as I should be, and I'm not always patient. But I know You've given me a way to project Your love, joy, patience, kindness, and other qualities. You've placed Your Holy Spirit inside me, and He helps me to bear the fruits You've listed in Your Word. Thank You, Lord, for Your Holy Spirit. Thank You that His work causes me to be the kind of man You've called me to be.

—————— THINK ABOUT IT: ——————

What character qualities do you believe God wants
you to demonstrate in your daily life? How does
God's Holy Spirit help you to bear those fruits?

FREE TO ACT IN LOVE

*But you must be careful so that your freedom does
not cause others with a weaker conscience to stumble.*
1 CORINTHIANS 8:9 NLT

Precious Savior, I thank You for setting me free from the power
of sin and death. Thank You that I am free to live without constant worry about what is right and wrong in Your eyes. You
let me know when I'm on the right track, and You let me know
when I need to make changes. But never let me forget that I
must make my life choices with an eye toward loving others—
especially my brothers in the faith. I never want to be a stum-
bling block to those with a more sensitive conscience or who
are prone to falling back into old sinful behavior.

THINK ABOUT IT:

*What behaviors can you think of that are not, in and of
themselves, sinful? How do you decide which of those you
should avoid in order to avoid making others stumble?*

WHEN GOD IS SILENT

How long, LORD, must I call for help, but you do not listen?
Or cry out to you, "Violence!" but you do not save?
HABAKKUK 1:2 NIV

Faithful God, there have been times in my walk with You when I've prayed fervently, consistently, and persistently over some important issue, but I felt like You weren't hearing me. In times like that, please give me the assurance that You haven't forgotten me—that You are still concerned over the issues that cause me to lose sleep. Help me to remember Your promise to hear my prayers when I call out to You. Lord, I don't know why You sometimes wait before You answer, but when You delay, please help me to continue trusting You.

THINK ABOUT IT:

When was the last time it felt like God wasn't hearing or answering your prayers? How did you handle it?

LIVING FAITH

What good is it, my brothers and sisters, if someone claims to have faith but has no deeds? Can such faith save them? . . . Faith by itself, if it is not accompanied by action, is dead.

JAMES 2:14, 17 NIV

Lord Jesus, You've promised me in Your written Word that my salvation is a gift from You, granted when I put my faith in Your work on the cross. But You also told Your followers that knowing You would result in good works, all of which glorify You as other people see that this faith is real and living. Lord, show me what good works You'd like me to accomplish today. You've already saved and transformed me, so please show me and others that my faith is real, by the good I do in Your wonderful name.

—————— THINK ABOUT IT: ——————

How do you believe your salvation and good works are related? How can you put your faith into action today?

MATURITY

He is the one we proclaim, admonishing and teaching everyone with all wisdom, so that we may present everyone fully mature in Christ.
COLOSSIANS 1:28 NIV

Father God, when I look back to the time You brought me to salvation and compare that new believer to who I am today, I can see that You've caused me to mature in my faith. If I do the same thing in another five years, I believe I'll see a much more mature Christian man than I am now. I know that Your will for me is to become fully mature in You and to help others who are on their own road to spiritual maturity. Lord, I know I'll only reach perfection when I'm with You in heaven—but until then, strengthen me daily as I continue to mature into the man of God You created me to be.

THINK ABOUT IT:

What can you do to keep yourself on your own road to spiritual maturity?

NO MERCY LIKE GOD'S MERCY

Who is a God like You, pardoning iniquity and passing over the transgression of the remnant of His heritage? He does not retain His anger forever, because He delights in mercy.
MICAH 7:18 NKJV

Gracious, merciful Father, thank You for loving me and for joyfully showing me mercy when I sin against You. I have known men who hang on to their anger long after someone has done them wrong, even when the other person apologizes. But You, Lord, are not like that. You don't retain Your anger, though You would be just in doing so. You not only let go of Your anger and grant mercy to those in need, You actually take joy in doing so. Thank You for delighting in showing me mercy.

THINK ABOUT IT:

How easy is it for you to show mercy to those who hurt or offend you? How is God different from humans when someone sins against Him?

POISONOUS PRIDE

Human pride will be brought down, and human arrogance will be humbled. Only the LORD will be exalted on that day of judgment.

ISAIAH 2:11 NLT

Lord God, I confess that I'm sometimes tempted to become prideful. I want to rule my own life instead of letting You take charge. I want to depend on my own skills and abilities instead of turning them over to You and letting You use them to bless me. And I want to decide what is right and wrong for myself instead of relying on what You've told me in Your written Word. But that Word repeatedly tells me that You oppose human pride and bless humility. Lord, humble my heart before You. Help me to rely on You and live for You in every way.

THINK ABOUT IT:

Why do you think God hates human pride so much? What can you do to keep yourself from the sin of pride?

FORGIVING AS GOD FORGIVES

*Bear with each other and forgive one another
if any of you has a grievance against someone.
Forgive as the Lord forgave you.*
COLOSSIANS 3:13–14 NIV

Lord Jesus, as You hung on the cross, bloodied and bruised from the beatings You had taken at the hands of Your executioners, You set an example for me. You showed what You expect from me when You said, "Father, forgive them, for they do not know what they are doing." I have a hard time understanding that level of forgiveness. In fact, I struggle to forgive those who have wronged me in even the smallest ways. But that's exactly what You tell me to do, Lord. You've forgiven me for my sins, and You command me to forgive those who sin against me. Please grant me a forgiving heart, for that is the only way I can obey Your command to forgive.

THINK ABOUT IT:

Do you find it difficult to forgive those who have wronged you? How important is it to God that you forgive others?

YOUR WORDS AND THOUGHTS

May these words of my mouth and this meditation
of my heart be pleasing in your sight,
Lord, my Rock and my Redeemer.
Psalm 19:14 niv

Precious God, I confess that my words and my thoughts aren't always of the kind that please You. Sometimes I think negative thoughts about others, including Your own people, and the negative words soon follow. Other times I speak words of complaint about other people's actions, and those words only reinforce my critical, negative thoughts. Lord, I know that my words and my thoughts are connected with one another, so I ask You to help me as I try to speak in ways that build others up—and think thoughts that focus on You and Your Word. I want to please You in all that I say and think.

THINK ABOUT IT:

What kinds of words and thoughts please God?
How can you change the way you speak and think?

PROPER NOURISHMENT

Anyone who lives on milk, being still an infant, is not acquainted with the teaching about righteousness. But solid food is for the mature, who by constant use have trained themselves to distinguish good from evil.
HEBREWS 5:13–14 NIV

Heavenly Father, nearly every waking hour I'm bombarded with images, music, television shows, and movies that can stunt my spiritual growth. Not only that, I can turn on my screens any time of the day and find unsound "Christian" teaching—teaching that doesn't align with Your written Word. Lord, You've walked with me since the day You brought me into Your eternal kingdom. I want more than anything to grow in my relationship with You, but I need Your help. Give me the wisdom to know what is good for me and what keeps me from growing in You.

THINK ABOUT IT:

How can you test the things you watch and hear to know if they benefit your walk with God?

YOUR PROVIDER

*Ask the LORD for rain in the springtime; it is the LORD
who sends the thunderstorms. He gives showers of
rain to all people, and plants of the field to everyone.*
ZECHARIAH 10:1 NIV

God my Provider, few things can stress an individual or a family more than money problems. Lord, I've found myself in a financial place where I wondered how I was going to cover the next month's expenses and then feed my family. Your Son, my Savior, taught that You're the Creator who always feeds the birds—and who values me far more than them. You have created me to relate with You as a son relates to his father, and a good father wants to provide for his children. You're aware of my needs, and You want to meet them. When I'm in a place of financial stress, help me to look beyond my circumstances and trust You as my Provider.

——— THINK ABOUT IT: ———

*What is your usual response when you feel
stressed or worried over money problems?*

OUR SOURCE OF WISDOM

*If any of you lacks wisdom, you should ask God,
who gives generously to all without finding fault, and it
will be given to you. But when you ask, you must believe
and not doubt, because the one who doubts is like
a wave of the sea, blown and tossed by the wind.*

JAMES 1:5–6 NIV

Lord, I believe it when You say You will generously give me wisdom when I ask for it. I face many life situations that require me to act wisely. Please give me the wisdom to act and speak in ways that glorify You and benefit those You've placed in my life. Today, I choose to trust You to keep Your promise—the promise to give me wisdom when I ask for it. I will leave the "how" up to You.

THINK ABOUT IT:

*What kinds of life situations do you face that require
you to act and speak with wisdom? How confident
are you that God will give you that wisdom?*

SUFFERING FOR JESUS

For you have been given not only the privilege of trusting in Christ but also the privilege of suffering for him.
Philippians 1:29 NLT

Lord, I don't like the idea of suffering for anything or anybody, including You. But my love for You and for others makes me willing to do just that when it is required. I know it's not likely that I'll experience the kind of trials the first-century Christians suffered. All the same, when I am called to suffer through twenty-first century trials and tests because of my faith, help me to see it as a blessed privilege. Help me to continue trusting in You so I can get through my difficulties in a way that glorifies You and helps others to see Jesus in me.

THINK ABOUT IT:

What kind of trials or suffering have you had to endure because of your faith in Christ? How did you respond to those situations?

STAYING STRONG

"Yet now be strong, Zerubbabel," says the LORD; "and be strong, Joshua, son of Jehozadak, the high priest; and be strong, all you people of the land," says the LORD, "and work; for I am with you," says the LORD of hosts.
HAGGAI 2:4 NKJV

Father, I thank You for always being there for me. I praise You for the wisdom to know when I need Your help and encouragement as I work to accomplish a task You've given me to do. I confess that I don't always turn to You first when the going is tough. Sometimes, I turn to others for strength and encouragement. But even though You've placed fellow believers in my life so we can strengthen and encourage one other, You want me to make Your presence my first source of everything I need to get the job done.

THINK ABOUT IT:

Where do you usually turn first when you need strength and encouragement to accomplish something God has given you to do?

AN ETERNAL INHERITANCE

I will open my mouth with a parable; I will utter hidden things, things from of old—things we have heard and known, things our ancestors have told us. We will not hide them from their descendants; we will tell the next generation the praiseworthy deeds of the LORD, his power, and the wonders he has done.

PSALM 78:2–4 NIV

Father in heaven, I want to work hard and manage my assets wisely so I can leave my kids some kind of inheritance. But more than that, I want to leave them an inheritance that lasts into their own eternity, by instilling in them a love for You. Strengthen and encourage me to do that by reminding me of the tangible ways You've already blessed me. Lord, show me how I can leave behind a legacy of godliness and love for Your Word.

THINK ABOUT IT:

What can you do to begin the work of instilling in your kids a love for God and His Word?

"LITTLE" SINS?

But now is the time to get rid of anger, rage,
malicious behavior, slander, and dirty language.
COLOSSIANS 3:8 NLT

Father in heaven, I confess that I sometimes think of behaviors
such as fits of anger, talking about others in a negative way, and
profanity as "little sins"—as if they're not as bad in Your eyes as
murder or adultery. Help me to change my thinking about the
sins listed in Colossians 3:8, and then help me to change my
behavior. Instead of being easily angered, I want to be a patient
person who repays evil with good. Instead of being a gossip, I
want to be a man who only speaks well of others. And instead
of speaking profanities, I want to be someone whose language
always glorifies You.

THINK ABOUT IT:

How do you think God sees outbursts of anger,
malicious gossip, or filthy language? What steps
can you take to remove those things from your life?

CONFESSION TO YOUR BROTHERS

Confess your sins to each other and pray for each other so that you may be healed. The earnest prayer of a righteous person has great power and produces wonderful results.

JAMES 5:16 NLT

Father in heaven, I confess that, like most men, I am not usually comfortable sharing my struggles and failures with others. I don't like making myself vulnerable, and I worry that my brothers in the faith would look down on me if they knew about my hidden sins. But You, in Your wisdom, tell me I should confess my sins to others so that they can pray for me and hold me accountable. Humble me, and help me to understand how important it is that I make myself accountable to my brothers in the faith.

THINK ABOUT IT:

Why do you think most men find it so difficult to confess their sins to other believers? How do you think that kind of confession helps you in your walk of faith?

WHEN YOU SIN

My dear children, I am writing this to you so that you will not sin. But if anyone does sin, we have an advocate who pleads our case before the Father. He is Jesus Christ, the one who is truly righteous. He himself is the sacrifice that atones for our sins—and not only our sins but the sins of all the world.

1 JOHN 2:1–2 NLT

God of grace and forgiveness, thank You for sending Jesus, Your only Son, to earth so that I can be forgiven for my sins. You have transformed my thinking and behavior, but I still do things I know don't please or glorify You. Thank You, Jesus, for pleading my case before the Father. Thank You for making me righteous in Your eyes, even after I blow it. And when I do sin, may I confess it and turn away from it quickly.

THINK ABOUT IT:

What does it mean to you to have Jesus Christ as your advocate when you sin against God?

GOD'S SPIRIT WITHIN YOU

"I will ask the Father, and he will give you another Advocate, who will never leave you. He is the Holy Spirit, who leads into all truth. The world cannot receive him, because it isn't looking for him and doesn't recognize him. But you know him, because he lives with you now and later will be in you."

JOHN 14:16–17 NLT

Lord Jesus, before Your death on the cross, You promised Your followers that God's own Spirit would reside within them as they undertook their mission to do what was humanly impossible. I need Your Spirit today and every day. Thank You that in any struggle I face, be it spiritual, emotional, or physical, I can rely on Your Holy Spirit to guide me, to give me wisdom, and to strengthen me. Without Him, I'm weak and powerless. But with Him, I can do anything and everything You've asked of me.

—————— **THINK ABOUT IT:** ——————

In what ways does the indwelling Holy Spirit benefit you as a follower of Christ?

TELL THE TRUTH

*Do not lie to each other, since you have
taken off your old self with its practices.*
COLOSSIANS 3:9 NIV

God of all truth, I'm so often faced with situations where it
seems advantageous to speak half-truths, white lies, or outright
lies—even to my own family or my brothers and sisters in Christ.
Help me to overcome the temptation to be anything less than
honest, especially when telling the truth hurts. Lord, I know
that You hate lies and that I will face consequences when I willfully speak untruths. But I also know that I glorify You and pre-
serve my earthly relationships when I speak only the truth. I
want to glorify You in everything I do and in everything I say, so
guard my heart and mouth from lies.

THINK ABOUT IT:

*In what kinds of situations are you tempted
to speak untruths? Why do you believe that
telling the truth is always the best choice?*

KEEPING THE PEACE

*Never repay evil for evil to anyone. Respect what is
right in the sight of all people. If possible, so far as it depends
on you, be at peace with all people. Never take your own
revenge, beloved, but leave room for the wrath of God, for it
is written, "Vengeance is Mine, I will repay," says the Lord.*
ROMANS 12:17–19 NASB

God of peace, I live among people who are as fallen and sinful as I am. That means they often do things that hurt or anger me—sometimes accidentally and sometimes on purpose. That fallen, sinful side of me wants to strike back at people who do me wrong. But I know that You call the redeemed, transformed side of me to forgive those who sin against me. Give me a gracious, forgiving heart so that I can overcome the temptation to seek vengeance.

——— THINK ABOUT IT: ———

*How can you best keep the peace when someone
has done something to hurt or offend you?*

A LIFE OF INTEGRITY

*Whoever walks in integrity walks securely,
but whoever takes crooked paths will be found out.*
PROVERBS 10:9 NIV

Lord Jesus, during Your time here on earth, You were the perfect example of integrity. You never compromised when it came to following Your Father's law, and You never wavered in doing what He had sent You to do. Make me more like You every day. You made me a new creation when You brought me into Your family, and I want You and the rest of the family to see me as a man of integrity. Help me to be someone who follows Your Word first and who never compromises on what You tell me is right. Help me to love and obey You with a pure heart and with an eye toward Your eternal kingdom.

THINK ABOUT IT:

*What do you think God means when
He uses the word integrity in scripture?
In what ways are you a man of integrity?*

SEEKING HELP

"You will surely wear out, both yourself and
these people who are with you, because the task is
too heavy for you; you cannot do it alone."
EXODUS 18:18 NASB

Father God, I sometimes feel overwhelmed when I think about the responsibilities You've given me. I want to serve You faithfully, I want to give my wife and children my very best, and I want to do my job in a way that pleases my employer and glorifies You. And that's just the very beginning of all You've given me to do. I sometimes feel like I need help, but I'm often reluctant to seek it out. Give me the wisdom and humility I need to reach out for help—both from my brothers here on earth and from You.

—————— **THINK ABOUT IT:** ——————

How do you respond when you feel like you are
wearing down because you have so much to do?
Who can you turn to when you need help?

GODLY EMPATHY

Rejoice with those who rejoice;
mourn with those who mourn.
ROMANS 12:15 NIV

God of compassion and comfort, You always know what is going on inside me. You know when I feel stressed or grieved, happy or sad. You know when I feel like just hiding away by myself, and You know when I'm at my sociable best. You know those things because You love me so personally. Thank You for loving me like that. Lord, help me to extend that kind of love to the people You've placed in my life. Give me a compassionate, empathetic heart, and make me sensitive to the needs of those around me. Help me to offer comfort to those who are grieving, words of encouragement for those who are enduring difficult times, and words of wisdom for those who aren't sure what to do. Finally, allow me the privilege of celebrating with those who are rejoicing.

THINK ABOUT IT:

How can you become more sensitive
to the needs of people in your life?

SEXUAL PURITY

For this is the will of God, your sanctification; that is, that you abstain from sexual immorality; that each of you know how to possess his own vessel in sanctification and honor.

1 THESSALONIANS 4:3–4 NASB

Gracious heavenly Father, You didn't save me and bring me into Your eternal kingdom so that I could just go my own way and do whatever feels good. Every day, the world I live in fires all kinds of sexual temptations my way, and sometimes I feel almost overwhelmed. When I am tempted sexually, remind me that my body belongs to You—and that I am to honor You in everything I do. Help me to control my mind and my eyes first so that I can say "yes" to intimacy with You and "no" to intimacy with anyone who is not my wife.

THINK ABOUT IT:

What concrete steps can you begin taking today to avoid sexual sin? How can you train your eyes and your mind toward intimacy with God first?

BECAUSE OF HIS MERCY

He saved us, not because of righteous things we had done,
but because of his mercy. He saved us through the
washing of rebirth and renewal by the Holy Spirit.
TITUS 3:5 NIV

Precious Savior, thank You for bringing me into Your eternal kingdom. You transformed me through the power of Your love and Your Holy Spirit. I know that You want me to do good works for Your kingdom and for other people. But those things happen *because* You've saved me, not so that I *can* be saved. There is nothing I do on my own to earn salvation from the consequences of my own sin. You've done it all, and because of that I've been reborn and renewed by Your Holy Spirit. Humble me and help me to focus on the fact that I'm saved only because of Your mercy.

THINK ABOUT IT:

What comes to your mind when you think of the word mercy?
How is your salvation linked to the good works you do?

LOVE IN ACTION

Dear children, let us not love with words
or speech but with actions and in truth.
1 JOHN 3:18 NIV

My loving Father, sometimes it's easy for me to speak kind, loving words but difficult to put my love for You and for others into action. Forgive me when I fail to produce acts of love and kindness, and help me to love not just with my words but with my deeds. It's not always easy for a man to speak kind words, but it's sometimes even more difficult to love through what we do. So please provide me with opportunities to truly love others in ways that help them and glorify You. I thank You for Your love for me, and I ask You to help me to spread that love to other people with a heart of pure love.

THINK ABOUT IT:

How can you best put your love for
God and for others into action today?

A FRIEND OF GOD

And the scripture was fulfilled that says, "Abraham believed God, and it was credited to him as righteousness," and he was called God's friend.

JAMES 2:23 NIV

Lord, I've never had a problem with thinking of You as the Creator, and I've come to a place where I think of You as a loving heavenly Father. But my *friend*? That one stops me every time. Your Word talks about the men You called Your friends, and most important of all, Your Son Jesus said of His followers, "I have called you friends, for everything that I learned from my Father I have made known to you" (John 15:15). Father, I believe You always keep Your promises, and that makes *me* Your friend. And You aren't just any friend but my *best* friend.

THINK ABOUT IT:

Have you ever thought of yourself as a friend of God? What makes a man God's friend?

CONTENTMENT

Now godliness with contentment is great gain.
For we brought nothing into this world, and it is
certain we can carry nothing out. And having food
and clothing, with these we shall be content.
1 TIMOTHY 6:6–8 NKJV

God of light, I confess that if I'm not careful, I can place too much attention on acquiring earthly wealth and possessions. Your Word never condemns financial or material gain, but it does tell me I should never place my desire for those things over my desire for You. Lord, You want me to live a life of godliness and contentment. You want me to focus on conduct, thoughts, and attitudes that reflect You best. Lord, let me be content with all You've given me. Please help me always to pursue You and the life You want me to live.

THINK ABOUT IT:

What does the word contentment mean
to you? How can you learn to focus first
on godliness instead of earthly wealth?

RESPONDING TO POWER

But when Daniel learned that the law had been signed, he went home and knelt down as usual in his upstairs room, with its windows open toward Jerusalem. He prayed three times a day, just as he had always done, giving thanks to his God.

<small>DANIEL 6:10 NLT</small>

Lord, sometimes I feel shocked at the lack of concern for You and Your standards in my culture. I am grieved when I see how people conduct themselves today. I see many things that bring me to a point of anger or fear. Please remind me not to dwell on my negative emotions, but to pray to You about those things that most concern me. Help me to pray for my culture, for my political leaders, and for those I know who desperately need Your touch.

THINK ABOUT IT:

How do you respond when you see things in the world that just aren't right? Do you ever find yourself feeling angry and grieved over them?

ASKING IN JESUS' NAME

"I will do whatever you ask in my name, so that the Father may be glorified in the Son. You may ask me for anything in my name, and I will do it."

JOHN 14:13–14 NIV

Lord Jesus, thank You for Your promise to do whatever I ask in Your name. I confess that if I'm not careful, the requests I bring can become self-centered. Please keep me focused on what glorifies my Father in heaven. Help me to pray for what I know is important to You. Lord, may I never come to You in prayer with selfish motives. May I present my requests in Your name for those things that help me to live the life You call me to live . . .so that You will be glorified in everything I do.

— THINK ABOUT IT: —

What do you think it means to pray in Jesus' name? How is God glorified when He answers your prayers in His Son's name?

SOFTENING THE HARD HEART

Sow for yourselves righteousness; reap in mercy;
break up your fallow ground, for it is time to seek the
LORD, till He comes and rains righteousness on you.
HOSEA 10:12 NKJV

Thank You, Lord, for the message of Hosea 10:12. It looks like advice for a farmer, but it makes the point that I should take time to earnestly seek You and ask if I've neglected You in any way. Lord, I need to grow in my faith, and the only way for that to happen is for me to soften my heart. Then, as I seek You in prayer and Bible reading, I can receive what You have for me. Thank You for hearing me when I ask You to show me those areas of my life in which I've neglected You.

THINK ABOUT IT:

Is there some area of life where you've neglected
God's guidance and control? How can you give
Him that guidance and control now?

HANDLING REGRETS

*"So I will restore to you the years that the
swarming locust has eaten, the crawling locust,
the consuming locust, and the chewing locust. . . ."*
JOEL 2:25 NKJV

Forgiving God, there are things in my past I'm not proud of, things that make me wince when I think about them. If I could go back to the time in my life before I knew You and do some things differently, I would. But You, Lord, have promised me that You can and do use everything, even my bad decisions in the past, for my good and Your glory. There's nothing I can do to change the past, but there's plenty You can do to teach me important lessons and give me wisdom to impart to others. Lord, remind me always that You are my Redeemer, including the Redeemer of my past.

--- THINK ABOUT IT: ---

*Do you have regrets over things you've done?
How do you believe God sees those things today?*

YOUR SOURCE OF POWER

"This is the word of the LORD to Zerubbabel: 'Not by might nor by power, but by my Spirit,' says the LORD Almighty."
ZECHARIAH 4:6 NIV

Almighty God, I confess that I have a big streak of self-reliance. Sometimes I feel like I can do what You've called me to do under my own power. But Jesus, You told Your followers that apart from You, we can do nothing. I know You can use my strengths and talents to accomplish big things for Your kingdom. But that can only happen when I bring all I am to You. Lord, I know You don't want to share Your glory with anybody, so help me to humble myself and come to You daily, knowing that I can't do anything without You.

THINK ABOUT IT:

Do you see yourself as a strong, competent, gifted man? How do those attributes glorify God and bring others into His kingdom?

LEADING BY SERVING

But Jesus called them to Himself and said, "You know that the rulers of the Gentiles lord it over them, and those who are great exercise authority over them. Yet it shall not be so among you; but whoever desires to become great among you, let him be your servant."
MATTHEW 20:25–26 NKJV

Lord of my life, the world's picture of a great leader is far different from Yours. Most people believe that a great leader should be a strong man who knows how to exercise his authority over others. You, however, told Your followers that a great leader is one who makes serving others his priority. I believe You've called me to lead others in some capacity. Help me always to remember that Your kind of leader is one who serves first.

—————— THINK ABOUT IT: ——————

What comes to your mind when you think of the word leader? How important is it to you to serve others as you lead?

THE SIMPLICITY OF SERVING GOD

O people, the LORD has told you what is good, and this is what he requires of you: to do what is right, to love mercy, and to walk humbly with your God.

MICAH 6:8 NLT

Heavenly Father, thank You for making things simple for me. I confess that I tend to make serving and loving You more complicated than You have. It seems like human beings can't just take You at Your Word—simply loving You and humbly walking with You in the way You've wanted us to since the very beginning. When I love You from my heart, the good You want me to do for You and others will flow from within me—it won't be a burden. Life is often difficult and complicated. I thank You that my walk with You doesn't have to be.

— THINK ABOUT IT: —

What does it mean to you to walk humbly with God? What does God mean when He tells you to do what is right and love mercy?

CLOTHED IN HUMILITY

*All of you, clothe yourselves with humility toward one another,
because, "God opposes the proud but shows favor to the
humble." Humble yourselves, therefore, under God's
mighty hand, that he may lift you up in due time.*

1 PETER 5:5–6 NIV

Mighty God, I confess that my human pride sometimes shows itself in how I interact with others. I know You call me to be a humble man, and I know You want that humility to demonstrate itself so that others can see it. Your servant Peter wrote that I should "clothe" myself in humility. That, Lord, tells me that every day I need to choose to wear humility—like a jacket. I need to willfully choose to treat others as more important than myself. Father, remind me to do just that every morning—and to make sure I never take off my jacket of humility during the day.

THINK ABOUT IT:

*What does it mean to you to "clothe"
yourself in humility toward others?*

WAITING FOR STRENGTH AND POWER

He gives power to the weak, and to those who have no might He increases strength. Even the youths shall faint and be weary, and the young men shall utterly fall, but those who wait on the LORD shall renew their strength; they shall mount up with wings like eagles, they shall run and not be weary, they shall walk and not faint.

ISAIAH 40:29–31 NKJV

God of power and might, I confess that I'm not always as patient as You call me to be. Sometimes, when I see a task that needs doing—even one You've specifically called me to accomplish—I can run out ahead and attack it rather than wait on You. But I've learned that when I do that, my strength quickly dries up and I burn out. Lord, give me the wisdom to wait for You to give me the go-ahead and the empowerment I need to accomplish something great for You.

THINK ABOUT IT:

What does it mean to you to "wait on the Lord"?

PERSEVERING IN PRAYER

He touched the socket of his hip; and the socket of Jacob's hip was out of joint as He wrestled with him. And He said, "Let Me go, for the day breaks." But he said, "I will not let You go unless You bless me!"

GENESIS 32:25–26 NKJV

God of all blessings, I am humbled and challenged when I read of Your servant clinging to You and refusing to let go until You blessed him. May I show that kind of persistence and perseverance as I seek blessings from You. Father, I know You want to bless me in all I do for You, for that is one of the ways You are glorified in me. May I never give up or become discouraged as I come to You and ask for what I know You want to give me.

THINK ABOUT IT:

What do you do when it feels like God is reluctant to bless you? Do you believe that He really wants to bless you?

A PERFECT EXAMPLE

"Whoever wants to become great among you must be your servant, and whoever wants to be first must be slave of all. For even the Son of Man did not come to be served, but to serve, and to give his life as a ransom for many."

MARK 10:43–45 NIV

Lord Jesus, You are the perfect example of a godly servant. You came to earth to do great things—to teach, to preach, and to rebuke those You knew were wrong. But more than that, You came to serve—and serve to the point of giving up Your very life so that others could live forever. I know, Jesus, that You want me to do great works for You. Let those things flow from my willingness to serve others first, just like You did.

THINK ABOUT IT:

Do you want to do great things for God's kingdom? What does Mark 10:43-45 tell you about the key to doing anything for Him?

PRAYING FOR EARTHLY AUTHORITIES

I urge, then, first of all, that petitions, prayers, intercession and thanksgiving be made for all people—for kings and all those in authority, that we may live peaceful and quiet lives in all godliness and holiness.

1 TIMOTHY 2:1–2 NIV

Father in heaven, I often feel reluctant to pray for those in authority in the world today, especially those I know don't hold to Your standards of godliness. Lord, I confess that this comes in a very real way from my forgetting two things: You are in control, and You can change the hearts of even the most rebellious man or woman. Forgive me for my lack of faith. May I obediently pray for those in places of authority and then let You take care of the rest.

THINK ABOUT IT:

What keeps you from praying for those in authority in today's world? Why do you think God wants you to pray for these people?

CLOTHED IN LOVE

Therefore, as God's chosen people, holy and dearly loved, clothe yourselves with compassion, kindness, humility, gentleness and patience.
COLOSSIANS 3:12 NIV

God of love, I confess that I don't always do a good job of demonstrating Your love to those around me—especially to those outside the faith. I sometimes think judgmental thoughts, and I don't always show kindness to those who don't know You. Instead, I can be proud, harsh, and impatient. Forgive me, Lord, and help me to be a better example of Your love. When men look down on me, let it be because I serve You with my whole heart, and not because I'm harsh and judgmental. Let others see a living, growing example of the kind of love You poured out on me, even before I knew You.

THINK ABOUT IT:

Do you think people see God's love in you? How can you become a more loving person, both to those outside the faith and to your brothers and sisters in Christ?

WORDS THAT HURT

Out of the same mouth come praise and cursing.
My brothers and sisters, this should not be. Can both
fresh water and salt water flow from the same spring?
JAMES 3:10–11 NIV

Father, I'm prone to speaking unkind, even harsh, words to and about others. The words I speak matter to You, and I know that You want me to speak only helpful, uplifting words—even when I'm telling another man a needed, painful truth. Please renew my mind daily so that my words toward others are uplifting and kind, not critical and hurtful. When I don't have anything good or helpful to say about another person, help me to hold my tongue. And if I've said anything to hurt another person, help me to seek forgiveness and restoration.

— THINK ABOUT IT: —

How can you overcome the temptation to speak
negatively of other men? What steps can you take
to fix the situation when you've said something
inappropriate to or about another person?

LIGHT AND STRENGTH

The LORD is my light and my salvation;
whom shall I fear? The LORD is the strength
of my life; of whom shall I be afraid?
PSALM 27:1 NKJV

Father God, I live in a world of darkness, a world that doesn't know You or honor You—and the results speak for themselves. At times I feel overwhelmed at this darkness, and it seems that nothing within me can overcome it. Lord, I need Your light to guide my way, and I need Your strength to help me withstand everything that the father of lies throws at me. In many ways, Satan holds dominion over this dark world. But You, Lord, have dominion over him—You are in control of all things. With You as my light and strength, I have nothing to fear in this life.

THINK ABOUT IT:

What kinds of things in this dark world frighten
or worry you? How does knowing God is with
you help you to overcome your fears?

THE OBJECT OF YOUR LOVE

Do not love the world or anything in the world. If anyone loves the world, love for the Father is not in them. For everything in the world—the lust of the flesh, the lust of the eyes, and the pride of life—comes not from the Father but from the world.

1 JOHN 2:15–16 NIV

Lord Jesus, You once told Your followers that no one can serve two masters—because one will always pull our love and attention away from the other. In 1 John 2, Your Word tells me that I can't love You and the world at the same time. I have to live in this world, Lord, but I know that I can't love its ways. May my love be focused on You alone, so that my heart is never divided. I don't want to be tempted to serve anyone or anything but You.

THINK ABOUT IT:

How can you keep the cares and temptations of this world from diminishing your love for God?

STANDING IN THE GAP

"I looked for someone among them who would build up the wall and stand before me in the gap on behalf of the land so I would not have to destroy it, but I found no one."

EZEKIEL 22:30 NIV

Holy Father, when I look around me and see the state of the world today, there are so many people who seem hopeless— due to their own choices or due to what has been done to them. But You are a God who delights in changing hearts and transforming lives. You are a God who saves the irredeemable and heals the hopelessly sick. Thank You for the privilege of begging Your mercy, forgiveness, and healing for those who can't or don't pray for themselves. Let me be a man who consistently stands in the gap on behalf of others.

THINK ABOUT IT:

Who do you know who needs a loving touch from God today? Are you willing to stand in the gap and pray for that person?

DELIVERED FROM DISCOURAGEMENT

The righteous cry out, and the LORD hears them; he delivers them from all their troubles. The LORD is close to the brokenhearted and saves those who are crushed in spirit.
PSALM 34:17–18 NIV

Father in heaven, I believe it when You tell me that You are with me, even when I have reason to feel down and discouraged. Lord, life here on earth is hard—and in some ways it's even harder for a man of God who is focused on hearing and obeying Your instructions for a life that pleases You. I want to be that kind of man, but there are so many pressures around me—so many barriers in my way. Thank You, God, for Your promise to be there for me, to hear me when I bring my discouragement and troubles to You.

THINK ABOUT IT:

What do you find discouraging as you try to live a godly life? How do you handle that discouragement?

A MATTER OF TRUST

*Trust in the LORD with all your heart and lean not
on your own understanding; in all your ways submit
to him, and he will make your paths straight.*
PROVERBS 3:5–6 NIV

God, it's not always easy for me to trust another person completely, because even the best people I know have moments when they prove themselves less than perfectly worthy. But it's not that way with You. Thank You, Lord, that I can always count on You. You have proven Yourself trustworthy, not just in the lives of all the saints before me, but in my own life as well. Help me always to remember Your trustworthiness, especially when I need encouragement, comfort, or direction. Help me to look beyond my own circumstances and trust You fully to guide and direct me.

THINK ABOUT IT:

*Why is it sometimes difficult to trust in the Lord
with all your heart? When has He proven
Himself trustworthy in your own life?*

GIVING AND RECEIVING

Give generously to them and do so without a grudging heart;
then because of this the LORD your God will bless you in all
your work and in everything you put your hand to.
DEUTERONOMY 15:10 NIV

Giving God, I confess that I'm not always the most generous giver. My lack of generosity is often based on fear—I want to hang on to what I have so I won't come up short when it's time to pay bills and buy the things my family needs. I know this demonstrates a lack of faith in You and in Your willingness and ability to keep Your promises. Forgive me, Lord! You tell me that when I give out of a pure heart of generosity, You will take care of me and bless me. Remind me often that You keep *all* Your promises.

THINK ABOUT IT:

What keeps you from giving when you see a need? How can
you develop a generous heart and learn to give freely?

QUALIFIED TO DO YOUR PART

*There are different kinds of gifts, but the same Spirit
distributes them. There are different kinds of service,
but the same Lord. There are different kinds of working,
but in all of them and in everyone it is the same God at work.*

1 CORINTHIANS 12:4–6 NIV

Father in heaven, You've called many people who didn't necessarily believe they were qualified to serve. I remember
Moses, who didn't think his status or oratorical skills were good
enough. Lord, I want to serve You and others, but I know I can
only do that when You empower and equip me. Show me what
You want me to do for You, and then, when I question whether
I am qualified to serve, remind me that Your Holy Spirit gives
me everything I need. You will empower me to make a difference in my congregation and in the world around me.

THINK ABOUT IT:

*What do you think qualifies you to serve
God in your church and in the world around you?*

LIVING IN CHRIST

*So then, just as you received Christ Jesus as Lord,
continue to live your lives in him, rooted and built
up in him, strengthened in the faith as you were
taught, and overflowing with thankfulness.*

COLOSSIANS 2:6–7 NIV

Lord Jesus Christ, thank You for coming to earth to live, die, and be raised from the dead so that I could be brought into Your eternal kingdom. But I confess that I am often torn: On one hand, I want to do what pleases me, but on the other, I want to live in a way that glorifies and pleases You. Help me to grow in my faith in You, my love for You, and my gratitude over all You've done for me. When these things fill my heart, my overcoming desire is to live for You and in You. Fill my heart, Lord.

THINK ABOUT IT:

What does it mean to you to live your life in Christ?

THE AMAZING POWER AND LOVE OF GOD

"Ah, Sovereign LORD, you have made the heavens and the earth by your great power and outstretched arm. Nothing is too hard for you."
JEREMIAH 32:17 NIV

Lord God, as a mere man I am severely limited in what I have the power to do. I can't change people's hearts, I can't arrange events in this world, I can't make the dead live, and I can't rescue anyone from the consequences of sin. But You can. You are my Creator—the Creator of the whole universe—and there is nothing You can't do. I can't fully comprehend Your incredible power. I stand amazed that a God of such might actually cares for such an insignificant creature as me. Thank You for being big enough and powerful enough to create all I see, yet kind and loving enough to reach down to me individually.

THINK ABOUT IT:

How can you know for certain that the all-powerful God cares for you on a personal level?

A BOOK I CAN TRUST

No prophecy of Scripture is of any private interpretation,
for prophecy never came by the will of man, but holy men
of God spoke as they were moved by the Holy Spirit.
2 PETER 1:20–21 NKJV

Thank You, God, for going to such amazing lengths to give me the Bible. I know I can trust Your written Word because Your own Holy Spirit inspired men of Your own choosing to write it. The words of this book reflect Your heart. They give me Your every promise, every command, and every bit of wisdom I need to live a life of faith that pleases You. I confess that sometimes I don't read Your Word as regularly as I should. Help me make time in Your Word a daily priority.

--- **THINK ABOUT IT:** ---

How important is daily Bible reading to you?
How can you make time to read the Bible every day?

"ONE ANOTHER"

And let us consider how we may spur one another on toward love and good deeds, not giving up meeting together, as some are in the habit of doing, but encouraging one another—and all the more as you see the Day approaching.
HEBREWS 10:24–25 NIV

Lord, Your Word repeatedly confirms how important it is that I spend time with other believers. You've put me in a circle of fellowship so that my brothers and I can love one another, encourage one another, serve one another, and challenge one another. Yes, there are times when it's just You and me, with no one else around. Those times are vitally important to me as I grow in my relationship with You. But I also need to spend time with other believers. Help me to train my mind toward giving and receiving blessings as I spend time with fellow followers of Christ.

THINK ABOUT IT:

Why is it important to God that you spend time with other Christians?

CONFIDENT REQUESTS

This is the confidence we have in approaching God:
that if we ask anything according to his will, he hears us.
And if we know that he hears us—whatever we ask—
we know that we have what we asked of him.

1 JOHN 5:14–15 NIV

Generous Father, Your Word tells me that You want to bless me, that You want me to have what I ask for in prayer. But You won't give me just anything I request—I must pray according to Your will as it is spelled out in scripture. When I know that what I'm praying for is Your will for me, I can approach You and pray with confidence, knowing that You want to do what I ask. Thank You, Lord, for giving me Your Word so that I can pray according to Your will.

THINK ABOUT IT:

How do you know for sure that God hears
your prayers? How can you know that what
you request in prayer is His will for you?

KEEPING A COOL HEAD

Don't be quick to fly off the handle. Anger boomerangs.
You can spot a fool by the lumps on his head.
ECCLESIASTES 7:9 MSG

God of peace, I try not to be a hot-headed man. But I confess that there are times when I lose my temper and do and say things that don't please You. Forgive me for my anger and help me to keep a cool head when someone provokes me, even unintentionally. Help me to respond to provocations in a loving way, but if I do become angry, help me to reconcile with the other person quickly. I know anger itself isn't a sin, but losing my temper is. And I don't want to dishonor You by displaying unrighteous anger.

THINK ABOUT IT:

What kinds of things can cause you to lose your temper?
How can you keep a cool head when someone provokes you?

A BLESSED INVITATION

*Then the angel said to me, "Write this: Blessed are those
who are invited to the wedding supper of the Lamb!"
And he added, "These are the true words of God."*
REVELATION 19:9 NIV

Lord Jesus, I've been to many weddings, and I've noticed something: While a wedding is a solemn ceremony in which two people vow to spend the rest of their lives together, it's also a festive occasion. The reception that follows is a time when friends and family members join the bride and groom to eat, drink, dance, and offer their congratulations. Lord, You've offered me a special invitation to the greatest wedding feast of all time. Not only that, I'll be one of the guests of honor! Help me to live daily in the assurance that I'll one day attend the party to end all parties.

—————— **THINK ABOUT IT:** ——————

*How can Revelation 19:9 assure you that you belong
to Jesus, today and forever? What do you think
the wedding feast of the Lamb will look like?*

TRUSTING ENOUGH TO GIVE

"Bring the whole tithe into the storehouse, that there may be food in my house. Test me in this," says the LORD Almighty, "and see if I will not throw open the floodgates of heaven and pour out so much blessing that there will not be room enough to store it."

MALACHI 3:10 NIV

Lord, You command me in Your Word to give generously, and You have promised me great blessings when I obey. Yet I often find it difficult to open my wallet and give toward Your continued work here on earth. I believe my reluctance to give has less to do with simple selfishness and more to do with a lack of trust in You to provide what I need to care for my family. Father, forgive me for my lack of generosity. Forgive me for not trusting You enough to give out of what You've given me.

THINK ABOUT IT:

What keeps you from generously giving to others and to God's work here on earth?

GOOD AND PERFECT GIFTS

*Every good and perfect gift is from above,
coming down from the Father of the heavenly
lights, who does not change like shifting shadows.*

JAMES 1:17 NIV

Perfect Father, You tell me in Your Word that You hate human pride—that You actively oppose those with arrogant hearts and minds. Lord, remind me often that every good thing I have and every good thing I accomplish in this life are the result of Your generosity toward me. The enemy of my soul wants me to believe that I should feel pride over my accomplishments. He wants me to feel pride in what I do, what I earn, and what I have. But all those things are gifts from You, my generous Father in heaven. Thank You for all these things and more.

THINK ABOUT IT:

*What kinds of things have you accomplished
or earned in this life? Who do you believe
deserves the credit for them?*

PRAY DAILY

And pray in the Spirit on all occasions with all kinds of prayers and requests. With this in mind, be alert and always keep on praying for all the Lord's people.
EPHESIANS 6:18 NIV

Loving heavenly Father, You have given me the wonderful privilege of coming to You in prayer for any person or life situation. You delight in hearing from me and doing the things I ask You to do in the name of Jesus. You love changing people's circumstances, and You love changing people's hearts even more. And You do these things when one of Your own people makes time to pray. Never let me forget how powerful a weapon prayer can be. May I pray every day, giving thanks and bringing my requests to You. Bring to my mind family members, friends, church leaders, and government representatives so I can pray for them. And especially move my heart to pray for people who need Jesus.

THINK ABOUT IT:

What situations or people has God laid on your heart to pray for today?

TRUE CONFESSION

"The Pharisee stood by himself and prayed: 'God, I thank you that I am not like other people—robbers, evildoers, adulterers—or even like this tax collector.' . . . But the tax collector stood at a distance. He would not even look up to heaven, but beat his breast and said, 'God, have mercy on me, a sinner.' "

LUKE 18:11–13 NIV

My Savior Jesus, it's ironic that You call me to be more like a man who was considered the worst of sinners during Your time on earth and less like a man people believed was among God's most devout servants. But the tax collector in Your story is just the kind of man You call me to be—a man who knows he needs Your mercy and forgiveness. Keep me humble, Lord, by reminding me often that I'm saved not because I avoid certain sins but because of Your amazing love.

THINK ABOUT IT:

How do you put yourself in position to receive God's mercy and forgiveness?

FAITH DEFINED

Now faith is confidence in what we hope
for and assurance about what we do not see.
This is what the ancients were commended for.

HEBREWS 11:1–2 NIV

Lord, I know that I can't please You without faith. I know that I must believe that You are and that You will reward me when I seek after You with everything I have. But sometimes I still have doubts. Sometimes I don't feel fully assured that You keep Your promises. Sometimes I feel like I need to see results before I fully believe. Father, help me not to become discouraged today but to continue trusting You and following You with everything I have. I will do that, trusting You to strengthen my faith and give me the assurance that You'll do what is best for me, even though I don't yet see it. Thank You for the gift of faith.

THINK ABOUT IT:

What does the word faith mean to you?
How do you handle your moments of doubt?

CREATED TO WORK

The LORD God took the man and put him in the
Garden of Eden to work it and take care of it.

GENESIS 2:15 NIV

Creator God, Genesis 2:15 tells me that You created me for a purpose: to work at accomplishing Your goals here on earth. Just as You put Adam in the Garden of Eden so he could work toward its upkeep, You've placed me where I work now to glorify You every day. Knowing that You created me to work gives the job I do, even the "secular" work, meaning and purpose. Empower me to glorify You as I labor, even when the tasks I'm assigned seem mundane. Thank You for giving me the ability to work and for allowing me to honor You as I do.

THINK ABOUT IT:

How does knowing that God created you to glorify Him in your work change how you approach your job? How can you honor Him daily, even if your work is of the "secular" variety?

A GOD OF MERCY

"O my God, incline Your ear and hear; open Your eyes and see our desolations, and the city which is called by Your name; for we do not present our supplications before You because of our righteous deeds, but because of Your great mercies."

DANIEL 9:18 NKJV

Merciful, gracious God, thank You that the favor You so generously pour out on me has nothing to do with my performance or worthiness and everything to do with who You are. I sometimes fall into thinking that it's the other way around—that You only answer my prayers and bless me when I show myself worthy. Remind me often that You extend Your goodness to me only because You are so merciful and compassionate. That way, You, not I, receive the glory. Thank You for who You are.

THINK ABOUT IT:

Why do you think God blesses you and hears you when you pray? Do you ever feel like you're not "good enough" to go to God in prayer?

SACRIFICING FREEDOM

"I have the right to do anything," you say—but not everything is beneficial. "I have the right to do anything"—but not everything is constructive. No one should seek their own good, but the good of others.

1 Corinthians 10:23–24 NIV

Loving heavenly Father, thank You for setting me free and allowing me to live in freedom. But even though I'm free from the bondage of living under a bunch of rules, I know I am to live my life in a way that glorifies You and benefits other men—believers and non-believers alike. Lord, give me a heart that is willing to sacrifice its own desires—even those that aren't necessarily sinful—for the good of my brothers in Christ and of those who don't yet know You.

THINK ABOUT IT:

What freedoms can you sacrifice daily for the good of others? How can you help others grow in their relationship with Jesus?

A HUMAN SUPPORT SYSTEM

*Two are better than one, because they have a
good return for their labor: If either of them falls
down, one can help the other up. But pity anyone
who falls and has no one to help them up.*
ECCLESIASTES 4:9–10 NIV

Lord, You never intended for me, or any other of Your followers, to make it through life alone. My relationship with You is
the most important in my life. But I need the fellowship and
companionship with other people—be it with my wife and other
family, my friends or fellow church members. I need people in
my life who will help pick me up when I'm down, and I desire
friends that I can pick up as well. Thank You, Lord, for putting
people in my life who act as my support system.

THINK ABOUT IT:

*Who in your life gives you support,
picks you up when you're down,
and encourages you when you need it?*

VICTORY OVER TEMPTATION

How can a young man cleanse his way? By taking heed according to Your word. With my whole heart I have sought You; oh, let me not wander from Your commandments! Your word I have hidden in my heart, that I might not sin against You.
PSALM 119:9–11 NKJV

Lord Jesus, I want to be able to say "no" to sin and "yes" to You. But the enemy of my soul throws so many temptations my way. I know I can have victory by storing up the truths of Your Word in my heart. You showed me how that works when You answered the devil's temptation with the Word of God. I know that Your Word is a powerful weapon in my war against sin. Remind me to wield it confidently when the enemy tempts me.

THINK ABOUT IT:

How can you best store God's Word in your heart so you can defeat temptations to sin?

CONFESSION AND CLEANSING

*If we claim to be without sin, we deceive ourselves
and the truth is not in us. If we confess our sins,
he is faithful and just and will forgive us our sins
and purify us from all unrighteousness.*

1 JOHN 1:8–9 NIV

God of righteousness, I've read Your written Word, and I know that all sin is a huge deal to You. You are completely holy and righteous, but You are also merciful and compassionate. I can't earn Your forgiveness, and there's no way I can repay You for it. Loving Father, I admit that I sin. Help me to see my sin as You see it, then bring it to You in confession. Lord, thank You for loving me in spite of my sins and imperfections. Thank You also for forgiving me when I simply confess my sins to You.

THINK ABOUT IT:

*What do you do when you realize you've sinned?
Do you run to God or away from Him?*

HEAVENLY TREASURES

"Do not lay up for yourselves treasures on earth, where moth and rust destroy and where thieves break in and steal; but lay up for yourselves treasures in heaven, where neither moth nor rust destroys and where thieves do not break in and steal. For where your treasure is, there your heart will be also."
MATTHEW 6:19–21 NKJV

Loving Savior, most men I know measure success in terms of what they can accumulate for themselves—the big bank account, the spacious home, the nice cars. But You have told me that those things will mean nothing when I enter into eternity. What will count then is how I've served You here on this earth. I know I need to work and earn a living in this life. But remind me daily to focus on storing up treasure—incorruptible, eternal treasure—with You in heaven.

—— **THINK ABOUT IT:** ——

What can you do to store up treasures in heaven?
What do you think those treasures will look like?

AN ETERNAL HOME

"My Father's house has many rooms; if that were not so, would I have told you that I am going there to prepare a place for you? And if I go and prepare a place for you, I will come back and take you to be with me that you also may be where I am."

JOHN 14:2–3 NIV

Lord Jesus, as You hung dying on a cross of wood, You took the time to offer an amazing promise to a penitent criminal: "Today you will be with me in paradise" (Luke 23:43). When I consider the fact that those words came from the Creator of the universe, my mind spins. What will my eternal home look like? Thank You for preparing a place especially for me, a place that will be an eternal paradise.

THINK ABOUT IT:

What do you think heaven will look like?
What will it be like to be with Jesus for all eternity?

THE RIGHT KIND OF BOASTING

"Let not the wise boast of their wisdom or the strong boast of their strength or the rich boast of their riches, but let the one who boasts boast about this: that they have the understanding to know me, that I am the LORD, who exercises kindness, justice and righteousness on earth, for in these I delight," declares the LORD.

JEREMIAH 9:23–24 NIV

Lord, remind me daily that I have nothing in and of myself to boast about. I know that even my understanding and knowledge of You come not from my own heart or mind but because I have Your Holy Spirit in me. When I boast, let me boast of You, never of myself. Let me boast of Your kindness and righteousness, which are the very reason You saved me in the first place.

THINK ABOUT IT:

What things are you tempted to boast about? What has God done for you that would cause you to brag on Him?

LOVING THE UNLOVABLE

If your enemy is hungry, give him food to eat; if he is thirsty, give him water to drink. In doing this, you will heap burning coals on his head, and the LORD will reward you.

Lord Jesus, You once asked Your followers, "If you love those who love you, what reward will you get?" (Matthew 5:46). The answer must have been "none"—because You wanted the disciples to understand that, as Your followers, they should do good for those who didn't love them in return. I confess that something inside me recoils at the thought of doing good for someone who won't appreciate it—someone who doesn't care about me. Lord, remind me every day that You call me to love everyone equally—even those who dislike or mistreat me.

THINK ABOUT IT:

How do you feel about loving someone who doesn't love you in return—or who just doesn't like you? In what ways can you love that person?

ASKING FOR A MIRACLE

Jesus said to him, "If you can believe, all things are possible to him who believes." Immediately the father of the child cried out and said with tears, "Lord, I believe; help my unbelief!"

MARK 9:23–24 NKJV

Lord Jesus, I've read the Bible stories of You performing amazing miracles during Your earthly ministry, and I've heard many modern-day stories of incidents that can only be explained as being Your work. I don't doubt for a minute that You have the power to perform miracles on behalf of people who cry out to You. Where I often struggle, though, is believing that You will perform a miracle for *me*. Thank You for loving me and making me one of Your own. I love You and believe You, Jesus, but help my unbelief. I need a miracle today.

THINK ABOUT IT:

Do you believe God can do great things in your life today? What keeps you from asking Him to perform a miracle for you?

THE PERIL OF LOVING MONEY

But those who desire to be rich fall into temptation and a snare, and into many foolish and harmful lusts which drown men in destruction and perdition. For the love of money is a root of all kinds of evil, for which some have strayed from the faith in their greediness, and pierced themselves through with many sorrows.

1 TIMOTHY 6:9–10 NKJV

Father in heaven, I've seen so many people destroy their lives, and the lives of others, by their love of money. Lord, You never condemned money itself as evil, and You actually encourage men to work hard to earn a living. But too many of us make money an object of love rather than a tool to care for our families and fund Your work. Empower me to work hard to earn, but keep my heart from the love of money.

THINK ABOUT IT:

How can you draw a line between wanting to earn a living and the love of money? How can you avoid crossing that line?

A HEART FOR FORGIVENESS

"For if you forgive other people when they sin against you, your heavenly Father will also forgive you. But if you do not forgive others their sins, your Father will not forgive your sins."
MATTHEW 6:14–15 NIV

My gracious heavenly Father, forgiveness is so important to You that You sent Your Son to earth to die so that my sins could be forgiven. Forgiveness is so important to You that You require me to forgive others before You forgive me. I confess that I sometimes have a tough time forgiving others. It's easy for me to hang on to offenses and dwell on them. Forgive me for my unforgiveness, and give me a heart like Yours—a heart that *wants* to forgive others when they do things that hurt or offend me.

THINK ABOUT IT:

Why do you think it's so important to God that His people forgive one another? What makes forgiveness so difficult for many people?

A LIVING SACRIFICE

And so, dear brothers and sisters, I plead with you to give
your bodies to God because of all he has done for you.
Let them be a living and holy sacrifice—the kind he will
find acceptable. This is truly the way to worship him.
ROMANS 12:1 NLT

Father in heaven, I confess that the idea of presenting everything—including my very physical body—to You can be frighten-
ing. I have to admit that I've often given You less of myself than
You deserve. I guess my fears come from the unknown. What
do You want to do with me? Where will You send me? What will
You ask me to give up for Your kingdom? Ease my apprehen-
sions and help me to focus on the fact that You love me and
want to bless me when I give my everything for Your use.

THINK ABOUT IT:

Are there parts of your life that you're reluctant to
give to God? What keeps you from completely
and wholly presenting yourself to Him?

KNOW YOUR ENEMY

Be alert and of sober mind. Your enemy the devil prowls around like a roaring lion looking for someone to devour. Resist him, standing firm in the faith, because you know that the family of believers throughout the world is undergoing the same kind of sufferings.

1 PETER 5:8–9 NIV

Father in heaven, thank You for giving me a heads-up about the enemy of my soul, the devil. He loves to use lies and temptations to distract and derail me in my walk with You. He knows that I am Yours forever, so now he works overtime to keep me from the work You've given me to do. Lord, give me the insight and wisdom to know when the devil is lying in wait for me, so I may avoid him and remain on-track for You.

THINK ABOUT IT:

What tactics do you believe the devil uses against you as you seek to do what God wants from you?

STRENGTH AND COURAGE FROM ABOVE

"Be strong and courageous. Do not be afraid or terrified because of them, for the LORD your God goes with you; he will never leave you nor forsake you."
DEUTERONOMY 31:6 NIV

Lord, sometimes I feel weak and afraid. Sometimes I'm overwhelmed, and I wonder how I'll ever truly enjoy the abundant life You've promised me. Life is often difficult, and it seems like the problems it throws my way are much too big for me. But I take courage in knowing that You are the all-powerful God who promises never to leave me to fight alone. While I'm limited in what I can do, nothing is too hard for You. I need the peace and the empowerment You've promised those who love and follow You.

THINK ABOUT IT:

Do you ever feel as though God has left you alone to face life's problems? How do you respond when you face a problem that seems too big?

THE TWO GREATEST COMMANDMENTS

He answered, " 'Love the Lord your God with all your heart and with all your soul and with all your strength and with all your mind'; and, 'Love your neighbor as yourself.' "
LUKE 10:27 NIV

Lord Jesus, You came to earth to bring a message of love. You demonstrated Your love for God and for people through Your words, Your actions, and even Your prayers. Your Word tells me that *my* love—love for You and for other people—isn't just to be emotional and verbal, but from the heart and accompanied by actions. Lord, I want to love God and other people the way You loved them. I want to live my life in a way that shows the true value of the two greatest commandments. May I reflect my love for You in everything I do, say, and pray.

———————————— **THINK ABOUT IT:** ————————————

In what tangible ways do you think God wants you to demonstrate your love for Him and your neighbors?

TEMPTED TO COMPROMISE

"If we are thrown into the blazing furnace, the God we serve is able to deliver us from it. . . . But even if he does not, we want you to know, Your Majesty, that we will not serve your gods or worship the image of gold you have set up."
DANIEL 3:17–18 NIV

Righteous Father, thank You for this example of men refusing to compromise on what they knew was right. I need their encouragement, because I live in a world that continually pressures me to do things that I know aren't right. When I am faced with a choice between honoring You or compromising my faith, give me the courage to stand for You. Lord, I will serve and obey You and You alone, even when it means encountering all sorts of difficulties.

THINK ABOUT IT:

Can you remember a situation in which you were pressured to do something you knew wouldn't please God? How did you respond?

KEEPING YOUR WORD

Above all, my brothers and sisters, do not swear—not by heaven or by earth or by anything else. All you need to say is a simple "Yes" or "No." Otherwise you will be condemned.
JAMES 5:12 NIV

God of truth, this world puts a lot of value on contracts and oaths. Many men seem to believe that their word means nothing unless it is prefaced with "I swear" or "I promise." Father, I know that's not how it should be with me. I want to be a man people can trust. I want to be a man of my word, a man who always does what he says he will do, a man who tells the whole truth, a man who sees his "Yes" and "No" as completely binding. Make me that kind of man.

THINK ABOUT IT:

Do you think others see you as someone who always keeps his word? What can you do to enhance or develop a reputation as a man whose words can be trusted?

JUST BEING THERE

*As iron sharpens iron, so a man sharpens
the countenance of his friend.*
PROVERBS 27:17 NKJV

Father in heaven, thank You for the Christian brothers You've placed in my life. These men mean the world to me, as they provide me with friendship and fellowship in You. I know You want me to remain "sharp," and I've seen how You accomplish that by using my friends to challenge, confront, and encourage me in my walk of faith. Remind me to tell them how much I appreciate the part they play in my walk of faith, and help us to submit to one another in a mutual relationship of encouragement and accountability. Make me the kind of friend who helps keep my brothers sharp in their walk of faith too.

--- THINK ABOUT IT: ---

*How do your Christian brothers help you
in your walk of faith? Can you think of
someone who needs some "sharpening"?*

THE PRIVILEGE OF PRAYER

"As for me, far be it from me that I should sin against the LORD in ceasing to pray for you; but I will teach you the good and the right way."
1 SAMUEL 12:23 NKJV

Faithful God, thank You for the gift of prayer. Prayer is a wonderful privilege for the man who loves You, but it's also my responsibility. You have called me to pray for everything that concerns me and everything that concerns You. You want me to pray for myself and my family, for my Christian brothers and sisters, for those who need Jesus, for my nation and its leaders, and anything else You lay on my heart. When I pray, You are moved to change situations and change hearts. Never allow me to neglect daily talks with You—or my listening to hear what You have to say in return.

THINK ABOUT IT:

How often do you go to God in prayer?
What kinds of things do you pray about?

GODLY LOVE

Love is patient, love is kind. It does not envy, it does not boast, it is not proud. It does not dishonor others, it is not self-seeking, it is not easily angered, it keeps no record of wrongs. Love does not delight in evil but rejoices with the truth.

1 Corinthians 13:4–6 NIV

God of love, You have called me to love others as You have loved me. I confess that I need Your help to love like that. I need to be more patient and kind, and I need to be more humble. I sometimes become angry at others when they don't treat me the way I think I deserve, and I hang on to that anger. Help me in these areas, Lord. Please start by making me less self-centered and more others-centered. Help me to love as You love.

THINK ABOUT IT:

In what areas do you believe you need to be more loving? How can you start loving better today?

HOW BIG IS YOUR FAITH?

"Truly I tell you, if you have faith as small as a mustard seed, you can say to this mountain, 'Move from here to there,' and it will move. Nothing will be impossible for you."
MATTHEW 17:20 NIV

Lord Jesus, I often wonder if I have enough faith—a big enough faith to believe You for the great things You've promised to do for me. So I remain stuck in the same place, afraid that You'll be offended at my small faith. But You tell me that I don't need a lot of faith to do great things for You, or to have You do great things for me. All I need to do is move out in the faith I have and ask. Remind me daily that the issue isn't the size of my faith but the greatness of my God.

THINK ABOUT IT:

Do you believe you have enough faith to dare to ask God for something great? What does Matthew 17:20 say about that?

SINFUL ANGER

"In your anger do not sin": Do not let the sun go down while you are still angry, and do not give the devil a foothold.
Ephesians 4:26–27 NIV

Righteous Father, nowhere does Your Word tell me that anger is sinful in and of itself. In fact, it tells me that even You sometimes feel righteous anger. Sometimes I get angry over the same things that anger You, but I also feel anger over what I consider personal insults or slights. Whatever the cause, please help me to handle my anger in ways that don't lead me to sin. When I'm angry over injustice or unrighteousness, help me not to cross the line and start hating the perpetrators. And when I'm angry for personal reasons, keep me from lashing out in any way. Instead, help me to quickly reconcile and make peace with those who have angered me.

THINK ABOUT IT:

At what point do you think anger becomes sinful?
How can you avoid sinful anger?

SEEING GOD'S CREATIVITY IN NATURE

"But ask the animals, and they will teach you, or the birds in the sky, and they will tell you; or speak to the earth, and it will teach you, or let the fish in the sea inform you. Which of all these does not know that the hand of the LORD has done this?"

JOB 12:7–9 NIV

Creator God, thank You for making such a beautiful universe, including the planet I live on. I enjoy seeing everything from a magnificent mountain range to a tiny hummingbird feeding from a flower. Lord, I don't literally see You when I'm hiking a nature trail, fishing at a free-flowing stream, climbing a mountain, or going birdwatching. But I can see something of Your character and Your creativity, and that makes the time I spend enjoying nature all the more special.

—————— THINK ABOUT IT: ——————

What can the beauty of the physical earth and the life that inhabits it teach you about the nature of God?

PLANTING THE RIGHT SEEDS

Do not be deceived: God cannot be mocked. A man reaps what he sows. Whoever sows to please their flesh, from the flesh will reap destruction; whoever sows to please the Spirit, from the Spirit will reap eternal life.
GALATIANS 6:7–8 NIV

Righteous God, You've arranged life on this earth so that a man's thoughts and actions have consequences. I know that if I live and think according to Your will, I'll see good results—and if I don't, I won't. Lord, I want to reap the harvest of eternal life—not just for myself but also for those You've placed in my life. Keep me mindful of the importance of living the way You've called me to live, and not in a way that pleases my own desires.

THINK ABOUT IT:

In what specific ways can you sow seeds that will produce a harvest of eternal life and reward? What kinds of seeds are you planting?

FORGIVEN!

How blessed is he whose wrongdoing is forgiven, whose sin is covered! How blessed is a person whose guilt the LORD does not take into account, and in whose spirit there is no deceit!
PSALM 32:1–2 NASB

God of forgiveness, I cannot thank You enough for forgiving my sins when I come to You in confession. You have assured me that when I confess my wrongdoing, You are faithful and just to completely forgive me and completely cleanse me. When You forgive my sins, You also choose to put them out of Your mind, casting them into a deep sea of divine forgetfulness. Lord, when I sin, move me to confess it quickly and turn away from it so that I can be clean before You.

THINK ABOUT IT:

How do you know for sure that God has forgiven your sins? What does it mean to you that God "does not take into account" your guilt?

IT'S NOT FAIL!

*In this meaningless life of mine I have seen both
of these: the righteous perishing in their righteousness,
and the wicked living long in their wickedness.*
ECCLESIASTES 7:15 NIV

Righteous God, I just can't figure out why bad things happen to good men while those who live unrighteous lives prosper from their misdeeds. To me, it seems right that a man who faithfully follows You would live a long, prosperous life. But it doesn't always turn out that way. Lord, in my limited human thinking, this seems unfair. But I know You have reasons for doing what You do. I don't ask for complete understanding of these things—I just ask that You would help me to trust Your perfect judgment and timing. Remind me that, in the end, You will set everything right.

THINK ABOUT IT:

Why do you think God allows bad things to happen to righteous people while the ungodly seem to prosper?

EQUIPPED TO DO GOD'S WILL

Now may the God of peace who brought up our Lord Jesus from the dead, that great Shepherd of the sheep, through the blood of the everlasting covenant, make you complete in every good work to do His will, working in you what is well pleasing in His sight, through Jesus Christ, to whom be glory forever and ever. Amen.
HEBREWS 13:20–21 NKJV

God of peace, thank You for sending Your Son to die for my sins. In Your awesome power, You raised Him from the dead and brought Him back to heaven to sit at Your right hand. Thank You for showing me Your will and for giving me good works to do here on earth. Thank You too, for equipping me and preparing me with all I need to faithfully and effectively serve You. Remind me daily to seek out Your power and strength.

THINK ABOUT IT:

What does it mean to you that God is "working in you what is well pleasing in His sight"?

A PROPER SELF-IMAGE

*For I say, through the grace given to me, to everyone
who is among you, not to think of himself more highly
than he ought to think, but to think soberly, as God
has dealt to each one a measure of faith.*

ROMANS 12:3 NKJV

Lord, it's often tempting to think more highly of myself than
You would have me think. You don't call me to think self-
abasing thoughts but to think of myself as simply a sinner who
is saved through Your Son's work on the cross. In light of that,
help me to remember that any good in me is on account of You
and You alone. Thank You for Your love and for bringing me
into Your eternal kingdom. May I always remember that the
glory for doing that isn't on account of me.

— THINK ABOUT IT: —

*What does it mean to "think soberly" about yourself?
How do you think God sees you as one of His children?*

PEOPLE PLEASING?

Am I now trying to win the approval of human beings, or of God? Or am I trying to please people? If I were still trying to please people, I would not be a servant of Christ.
GALATIANS 1:10 NIV

Faithful God, I know that I can glorify You as I try to please certain other people—my wife, my boss, and those in authority over me. But I confess that I sometimes find myself trying to please other people with speech and behavior that doesn't please You. When I hear others speaking in ways I know aren't right, it's easy to join in to fit in. Father, forgive me for my lack of faithfulness to You and Your Word. Give me a heart and mind that are focused on pleasing You, not other men, first.

THINK ABOUT IT:

In what ways do you find yourself trying to please people? How can you make sure the way you live, speak, and think pleases God first?

RESTORING A BROTHER

Brothers and sisters, if someone is caught in a sin, you who live by the Spirit should restore that person gently. But watch yourselves, or you also may be tempted. Carry each other's burdens, and in this way you will fulfill the law of Christ.
GALATIANS 6:1–2 NIV

God of forgiveness, I'm not always comfortable speaking words of correction, even when I know my brother in the faith needs to hear them. Give me the courage I need to speak up when necessary, and the wisdom to choose my words carefully. I don't want to come off as condemning, so give me a gentle spirit to speak words of encouragement and restoration when my brother has gone off course. Help me never to forget that if I'm not careful, I can stray off course myself.

THINK ABOUT IT:

How should you respond when you know your Christian brother is in sin? How can you make sure your words reflect gentleness and restoration?

LOVING THE UNLOVING

"But love your enemies, do good to them, and lend to them without expecting to get anything back. Then your reward will be great, and you will be children of the Most High, because he is kind to the ungrateful and wicked."

LUKE 6:35 NIV

Lord Jesus, You set the perfect example of loving those who hated You and of giving everything to those who, like me, had nothing to give in return. I confess that I struggle with loving those who don't love me in return, and with doing good for them. But You never commanded Your followers to do something You weren't willing to do Yourself. So You always empower us to do as You have said. Help me to be kind and loving to those who show no kindness in return. When I do that, I'll be doing just like You did when You came to earth.

THINK ABOUT IT:

How can you show love and kindness to those who can't or won't reciprocate?

OPEN LINES OF PRAYER

"And when you stand praying, if you hold anything against anyone, forgive them, so that your Father in heaven may forgive you your sins."

MARK 11:25 NIV

Faithful, forgiving God, I never want anything to come between us. I never want to feel as if my line of communication with You is broken or damaged in any way. I know You want me to forgive those who have hurt or offended me—even if they don't confess their wrongdoing—and I know that my lack of forgiveness can keep You from hearing me. Help me to freely forgive so that You can forgive me and hear and respond to my prayers. If I'm harboring bitter or angry feelings against anyone, bring them to my mind so that I can forgive that person today.

THINK ABOUT IT:

How do you respond when you feel that your lines of communication with God are broken? Who do you need to forgive for wrongs done against you?

TRUE FRIENDSHIP

*Better is open rebuke than hidden love. Wounds from
a friend can be trusted, but an enemy multiplies kisses.*
PROVERBS 27:5–6 NIV

Father in heaven, You've given me some good friends, and I'm grateful for that. I'm especially close to a few of those men, so close that we're able to challenge one another, encourage one another, and even rebuke one another when needed. It's not easy to speak tough truths to anyone, even those I'm closest to, and it's harder still when my friends speak those tough truths to me. But I need that kind of friend. I need men in my life who care enough to speak honestly when they see I'm going off track. Thank You for those friends. Help me to *be* that kind of friend.

THINK ABOUT IT:

*How would you respond if you saw that your best friend
was straying from God? Do you have a close friend who
will rebuke you and speak correction when you need it?*

GROWING STRONGER THROUGH SUFFERING

Not only so, but we also glory in our sufferings, because we know that suffering produces perseverance; perseverance, character; and character, hope. And hope does not put us to shame, because God's love has been poured out into our hearts through the Holy Spirit, who has been given to us.

ROMANS 5:3–5 NIV

Father in heaven, I confess that when I'm going through difficulties, my mind doesn't automatically go to the good You can grow in me as I endure. But Your Word promises that I can take heart when I'm suffering because my own difficulties help me to develop a stronger, more consistent faith. While You never called me to enjoy life's difficulties, You have told me that I can rejoice in them—for they can increase my faith and draw me closer to You.

THINK ABOUT IT:

How do you usually respond when you're going through times of suffering? How can difficulties draw you closer to God?

SPIRITUAL TRAINING

*For physical training is of some value, but godliness
has value for all things, holding promise for both
the present life and the life to come. This is a
trustworthy saying that deserves full acceptance.*
1 TIMOTHY 4:8–9 NIV

Father in heaven, thank You for giving me my physical body. I know You want me to take care of it so that I can live a healthy life and serve You better. Help me to focus not just on my physical health but on my spiritual health as well. As I care for my inner man so that I can be more and more godly every day, show me what is beneficial to read, view, listen to, and talk about. Turn my attention toward those things, and away from the things that bring me down. Above all, never let me neglect spending time in Your presence.

THINK ABOUT IT:

*How can you best train yourself in godliness?
What are the benefits of this kind of training?*

GOD'S PLANS FOR YOU

"For I know the plans I have for you," declares the LORD,
"plans to prosper you and not to harm you,
plans to give you hope and a future."
JEREMIAH 29:11 NIV

Loving Father, many men love to make plans. We plan for our families, for our professional pursuits, and even for our spiritual ministries. As I make my plans, though, help me to remember that You already have my future mapped out. Give me an ear to hear what You've said about Your plans for me, and a pliable heart and mind so that I can adjust my plans to align with Yours. Give me the inner peace that comes from knowing that You love me and that You will never steer me wrong.

——— THINK ABOUT IT: ———

How does knowing that God has a plan for
your future affect your planning for yourself?

GOD'S WILL FOR YOU

Rejoice always, pray without ceasing, in everything give thanks; for this is the will of God for you in Christ Jesus.

1 THESSALONIANS 5:16–18 NASB

Father in heaven, thank You for giving us clear instructions on Your will in 1 Thessalonians 5. But I confess that rejoicing always, praying without ceasing, and giving thanks in everything don't come easily to me. In fact, there are times when I don't feel like doing *any* of these things. You don't call me to live by my feelings, though, but by faith in You. That, Lord, is Your will for me. So help me to focus not on my circumstances but on You and Your blessings to me. Remind me often how important it is that I consistently come to You in prayer.

THINK ABOUT IT:

How can you consistently rejoice, pray, and give thanks when you don't feel like it? Why is it so important to God that you do these things?

HEARING AND DOING

But don't just listen to God's word. You must do what it says. Otherwise, you are only fooling yourselves.

JAMES 1:22 NLT

Lord my God, I confess that I don't always act on what I read in Your written Word. Sometimes, I see some great truth but then go about my day as if I have no idea what I've read. Please forgive me. I know You want me to read from the Bible every day, but I also know it's even more important that I act on what I've read. Your written Word is filled cover-to-cover with wisdom and commands. But they won't mean a thing to me unless I obey. Through Your Spirit, make the Word come alive to me so that I can do what it says.

—————— **THINK ABOUT IT:** ——————

What can you do to make God's Word come alive in you? How can you make sure that you don't just hear His Word, but also do what it says?

AN ANTIDOTE TO WORRY

Do not be anxious about anything, but in every situation, by prayer and petition, with thanksgiving, present your requests to God. And the peace of God, which transcends all understanding, will guard your hearts and your minds in Christ Jesus.

PHILIPPIANS 4:6–7 NIV

My precious Lord, I confess that I'm sometimes given to worry. I worry about things most men feel anxious about these days, but I know it's not Your will that I lose sleep and get my guts in a knot over things I can't control. You want me to live in the peace that comes from knowing that You are in control and that You care for me and the people I love. May I always come to You first when I face a situation that causes me to worry.

THINK ABOUT IT:

What kinds of things worry you? How does knowing that God is in control of all things affect how you handle them?

COMPASSION AND FORGIVENESS

Be kind and compassionate to one another,
forgiving each other, just as in Christ God forgave you.
EPHESIANS 4:32 NIV

Loving Father, it was with great compassion and love that You reached down to me and welcomed me into Your heavenly kingdom. I didn't deserve it—You did it because of who You are. You've told me that I am to extend that same kind of compassion and forgiveness to those who sin against me. I confess that it's not in my nature to respond to others that way. I feel as if I'm entitled to hang on to anger, especially against those who hurt me intentionally. Lord, forgive me for my lack of compassion and for my unforgiving heart. Help me to forgive not because someone deserves it, but because it's part of who I am in You.

--- THINK ABOUT IT: ---

What keeps you from forgiving those who hurt you,
be it intentionally or unintentionally? How can you
become a more compassionate, forgiving man?

SECURE IN GOD'S LOVE

*"The LORD your God is with you, the Mighty
Warrior who saves. He will take great delight
in you; in his love he will no longer rebuke you,
but will rejoice over you with singing."*

ZEPHANIAH 3:17 NIV

Loving heavenly Father, so often I wonder how a holy God like You can take any pleasure in a man like me. I wonder how You can love me and take delight in me—how You could possibly take such joy in me that You would actually *sing* over me. But You not only promise to save me and be with me always, You tell me that You joy in me as Your own son. When I feel insecure in my relationship with You, remind me that You are tender and affectionate in Your fatherly love.

--- **THINK ABOUT IT:** ---

How do you think God sees you and feels about you? What do you do when you feel doubts about His affectionate love for you?

GOD'S PERFECT TIMING

*The Lord isn't really being slow about his promise, as some
people think. No, he is being patient for your sake. He does not
want anyone to be destroyed, but wants everyone to repent.*

2 PETER 3:9 NLT

Sovereign God, Your timing isn't like my timing. You exist and
rule outside of any human time constraints, and You alone control the timing of all the events leading to Christ's return. I want
Him to come back soon to set all things right and establish His
eternal kingdom. But You, being the perfect example of love,
wait—because You want to give all people a chance to turn to
You. Help me to live my life here on earth as if Jesus won't
return in my lifetime but also to work and live as if He's coming
back today. Either way, You win—and so do I.

THINK ABOUT IT:

*How can the phrase "He does not want anyone
to be destroyed" motivate you to speak
the truth of God's Gospel message?*

FOOLISH ARGUMENTS

*Don't have anything to do with foolish and stupid
arguments, because you know they produce quarrels.
And the Lord's servant must not be quarrelsome but
must be kind to everyone, able to teach, not resentful.*

2 TIMOTHY 2:23–24 NIV

God of peace, many of us enjoy a good debate, and I know You want men to stand for Your true Gospel. Your written Word doesn't tell me to avoid controversies at all cost. You call me to contend for the faith, to stand against bad teaching, and to speak the truth in love. But I need Your wisdom as I do these things. Help me to know when to speak up and when to hold my tongue. And above all, help me to avoid useless arguments over things that aren't important. May I always speak gently and lovingly to those who need to hear Your truth.

—————— **THINK ABOUT IT:** ——————

*How can you determine what is worth arguing or
debating, and what you should just leave alone?*

CHRIST LIVING IN YOU

I have been crucified with Christ; it is no longer I who live, but Christ lives in me; and the life which I now live in the flesh I live by faith in the Son of God, who loved me and gave Himself for me.

Galatians 2:20 NKJV

Lord Jesus, I want to live like You lived, love like You loved, give like You gave, and forgive like You forgave when You were here on earth. I want to be an imitation of You in all these ways and more, but my own desires often get in the way. Help me to deny myself daily, to take up my cross and follow You. I can only do that by faith in You, so help me to so fully trust and believe You that my life looks more like Yours every day.

THINK ABOUT IT:

What do you think "Christ living in you" would look like? What are the benefits of living a life of faith in the Son of God?

RUNNING UNENCUMBERED

Therefore, since we are surrounded by such a great cloud of witnesses, let us throw off everything that hinders and the sin that so easily entangles. And let us run with perseverance the race marked out for us, fixing our eyes on Jesus, the pioneer and perfecter of faith.
HEBREWS 12:1–2 NIV

Father God, just as a distance runner wouldn't want to start his race carrying a heavy pack, I don't want anything hindering me as I run my race of faith. Lord, please reveal to me anything that could possibly slow me down or trip me up, and then give me the strength and perseverance it will take to finish strong. Above all, help me keep my focus on Jesus and Him alone. Thank You, Lord, for inviting me to take part in the race.

THINK ABOUT IT:

What in your life right now could hinder you in your race of faith? What can you do to keep your eyes fixed on Jesus?

GOD'S OWN WORDS

All Scripture is God-breathed and is useful
for teaching, rebuking, correcting and training
in righteousness, so that the servant of God may
be thoroughly equipped for every good work.
2 TIMOTHY 3:16–17 NIV

Father, thank You for speaking through the people who wrote the scriptures. You use their words to help me know You better and to provide me all I need to be equipped to live a life that pleases You. I know I should focus on all of scripture, not just my favorite passages or verses, for the whole Bible is Your communication with me. Your Word is trustworthy, and it contains everything I need to know about You and Your will for my life. Your Word is useful to me because it prepares me to do what You have called me to do.

--- **THINK ABOUT IT:** ---

How do you go about finding the wisdom
you need from the Word of God? Have you
read the whole Bible, cover to cover?

NOBLE CHARACTER

*A wife of noble character who can find? She is worth
far more than rubies. . . . Her children arise and call her
blessed; her husband also, and he praises her: "Many
women do noble things, but you surpass them all."*
PROVERBS 31:10, 28–29 NIV

Blessed Father, my life is so busy, and sometimes I neglect the basics of family life, such as speaking uplifting, encouraging words to my wife. She is a blessing to me, so I want to make it a point not just to treat her with respect and love, but also to compliment her for who she is and what she does for me. Remind me to tell my wife every day how much I love her, value her, and appreciate everything she does for me, for our children, and for others.

--- THINK ABOUT IT: ---

*What keeps you from verbally praising your wife
for all she does and for who she is? How can you best
remember to speak encouraging, uplifting words to her?*

CUTTING WORDS

Some people make cutting remarks,
but the words of the wise bring healing.
PROVERBS 12:18 NLT

Lord, sometimes it seems like my Christian brothers and I spend more time making cutting, sarcastic remarks to one another—remarks we don't really mean—than we do speaking words of healing and encouragement. My friends are important to me, and I know they are a blessing from You. Help me to be careful not to go too far when I'm teasing them, but even more than that, give me uplifting, encouraging, healing words to speak to them. And when I'm frustrated or angry with someone, help me to check my words so that I don't say anything that cuts down that person. Give me the wisdom to know what I should and should not say.

THINK ABOUT IT:

What kinds of things do you and your friends say
to one another? How can you make it a point to
speak healing, encouraging words to them?

EARTHLY AUTHORITY

*Let everyone be subject to the governing authorities,
for there is no authority except that which God has
established. The authorities that exist have been established
by God. Consequently, whoever rebels against the authority
is rebelling against what God has instituted, and those
who do so will bring judgment on themselves.*

ROMANS 13:1–2 NIV

Lord of lords, thank You for placing people in positions of authority so they can keep order in the world. I know that You have appointed those rulers, even those with whom I disagree. Father, I know that You want me to live in obedience to earthly law, as long as doing so doesn't cause me to disobey You. Help me to know the difference between laws that encourage me to compromise and those that don't.

THINK ABOUT IT:

In what small ways might you be rebelling against earthly authority? How do you respond to earthly authority when you know it goes against what you believe as a Christian?

CHOOSING FRIENDS WISELY

*Do not be misled: "Bad company
corrupts good character."*
1 CORINTHIANS 15:33 NIV

Loving Savior, I know You want me to reach others for You by living out my faith before them. But I also know that I need to be wise in choosing the people I spend my time with, because if I'm not careful, I could be led into compromising situations. I need Your wisdom in this part of my life. I need You to guide my steps as I make my way through a world full of people who need You but who would not make good, close friends for me. Open my eyes to see who should be a good friend, while helping me to avoid compromise.

THINK ABOUT IT:

*How should you choose your close friends?
How can you avoid spending too much time
with those who may lead you into compromise
while at the same time modeling Jesus for them?*

SEEING GOD AS HE IS

Return to the LORD your God, for he is gracious and compassionate, slow to anger and abounding in love, and he relents from sending calamity.

JOEL 2:13 NIV

Righteous God, You identify Yourself in the Bible as a holy God who does not tolerate sin. But that's only part of who You are. You are also a gracious, loving heavenly Father who extends compassion and patience to me. Father, I confess that I don't always see the complete picture of who You really are. You are perfect in Your holiness, and You must deal with my sin. But You are also perfect in Your love, so You offer me mercy and forgiveness. Lord, help me to keep sight of You as You are: as a holy and righteous God but also as my gracious, compassionate, loving heavenly Father.

THINK ABOUT IT:

What comes to mind first when you think of God: His holiness and righteousness, or His love, patience, and compassion?

DOING GOOD

Who is going to harm you if you are eager to do good?
But even if you should suffer for what is right, you are
blessed. "Do not fear their threats; do not be frightened."
1 PETER 3:13–14 NIV

Father in heaven, I am eager to do what is right in Your eyes. Make me even more so. I want to bless You and other people through my actions. Please show me how. Help me to look past my fear of suffering for doing what is right and instead focus on You and the blessings You promise for obedience. Make it all about loving You and other people, and not about fear. Lord, I commit myself to doing good for You and for others, and to leaving the results in Your hands.

THINK ABOUT IT:

How do you handle fear over doing what is
right in God's eyes? What blessings do you
receive for doing good for God and others?

WHEN AN ENEMY FALLS

*Do not gloat when your enemy falls; when they stumble,
do not let your heart rejoice, or the LORD will see and
disapprove and turn his wrath away from them.*
PROVERBS 24:17–18 NIV

Lord, I confess that I'm tempted to feel at least a twinge of joy when a business adversary, a political leader I don't like, or some other opponent falls. That's especially true when that person has treated me in a way I don't think is right. Jesus, You told Your followers to pray for their enemies, not to wish ill on them. Please guard my heart from feeling pleasure or joy when my adversaries suffer or fail. Instead, remind me to pray for those people at all times, knowing that You will deal with them as You see fit.

— THINK ABOUT IT: —

*Have you ever felt satisfaction or pleasure
when someone you know fell on difficult times?
What do you believe God thinks of that attitude?*

HUMBLE BEGINNINGS

*Then the LORD took me as I followed the flock, and the
LORD said to me, "Go, prophesy to My people Israel."*
AMOS 7:15 NKJV

Father God, You don't always use the most highly educated or
credentialed men to accomplish Your purposes. Instead, You
often choose men of the most humble backgrounds. I think of
Amos, a farmer, and Moses, a shepherd. Then there was the
carpenter Joseph, the man You chose to be Jesus' earthly
father. And the apostles Peter, James, and John were all fisher-
men. You use the humble, the willing, and those who have the
courage and faith to say, "I'm here and available, Lord. Use me
as You will!" Though I may not have an impressive background,
I know You can do the same with me.

── THINK ABOUT IT: ──

*Do you ever feel unworthy for God's use because you
lack the education or credentials other men possess?
What makes a man worthy for God's service?*

THE MEASURE OF A MAN

Better is the poor who walks in his integrity than
one perverse in his ways, though he be rich.

PROVERBS 28:6 NKJV

Lord, in this world, people often judge a man by what he earns or possesses. Those with the biggest bank accounts and houses are seen as the ones to be admired. But You don't measure a man that way. You see into my heart and are most concerned that I am a man of integrity, that my thoughts and behavior reflect You in every way. You love integrity! Thank You, Father, that You don't measure me in terms of what I earn, what I own, or what I've accomplished. Instead, You measure me in terms of the good character You've instilled in me.

THINK ABOUT IT:

Do you ever find yourself looking up to other men based
on their income and status? Do your thoughts and
actions align themselves with your profession of faith?

A TRUSTWORTHY HEAVENLY FATHER

See what great love the Father has lavished on us, that we should be called children of God! And that is what we are!

1 JOHN 3:1 NIV

Father God, You have repeatedly identified Yourself in scripture as a loving heavenly Father, one I can fully trust to love me as a valued son. Some men struggle with the idea of the Creator of the world also being a loving Father—maybe because their earthly fathers were not good models of what love should look like. But Your love is far deeper and broader than that of even the best earthly father. You are perfect in every way, including in Your love for Your children. Thank You for being a loving heavenly Father—*my* loving heavenly Father.

THINK ABOUT IT:

Do you ever struggle with the idea that God isn't just your Lord but also your loving heavenly Father? What are some ways God has demonstrated His love to you?

CALLING ON GOD

The LORD is close to all who call on him,
yes, to all who call on him in truth.
PSALM 145:18 NLT

Loving Father, sometimes I feel a deeper need than usual to cling to the promise of Psalm 145:18. You tell me that You're near me when I call, but sometimes it doesn't feel that way. I don't enjoy those times when I feel like You're distant—but I also know those times are valuable because they cause me to look inside myself to make sure I'm calling on You "in truth." Lord, I call out to You today, believing the promise that You will draw close to anyone who calls on You from a pure heart. Thank You for Your love and for Your promise to stay close to me.

――――――――――――― THINK ABOUT IT: ―――――――――――――

What does it mean to you to call on God "in truth"?
What do you do when you feel like God is far away?

AN ALWAYS-PRESENT GOD

*Where can I go from your Spirit? Where can I
flee from your presence? If I go up to the heavens,
you are there; if I make my bed in the depths, you are there.*

PSALM 139:7–8 NIV

Lord, I'm grateful that there is nowhere I can go and nothing I can do to escape Your presence. You'll never leave me on my own because You love me on such a deep, personal level. Even in those times when I feel like I'd like to be by myself a while, You are there. During those times when I don't feel Your presence, You are there. When my life circumstances cause me to wonder if You have abandoned me, You are there. Even when I am tempted to sin—even when I give in to that temptation—You are there, drawing me back to You.

—— THINK ABOUT IT: ——

*Have you ever felt like you'd like to spend
time away from God's presence? What do
you think makes you feel that way?*

WALKING AS JESUS WALKED

*Whoever keeps His word, in him the love of God
has truly been perfected. By this we know that we
are in Him: the one who says he abides in Him ought
himself to walk in the same manner as He walked.*

1 JOHN 2:5–6 NASB

Jesus, thank You for coming to earth and giving us the perfect example of how to live every day. I've personally known men who lived godly lives, but nobody did it better than You. You lived selflessly, but You also knew You needed time alone with Your Father. You reached out to sinners in the most personal way, but You never compromised on what was right. And You sacrificed everything, including Your very life, so that I could be drawn into Your heavenly family. Help me to walk like You, Jesus!

THINK ABOUT IT:

*What do you think it means to "walk in the same
manner" as Jesus walked? How can you follow
Jesus' example of godly living today?*

THE GOOD NEWS

*How then will they call on Him in whom they have
not believed? How will they believe in Him whom they
have not heard? And how will they hear without a
preacher? How will they preach unless they are sent?
Just as it is written, "How beautiful are the feet of
those who bring good news of good things!"*

ROMANS 10:14–15 NASB

Savior and Lord, I'm amazed at how many people don't really understand who You are. They may know that You taught some great truths about life. They may even know that You claimed to be the Savior. But they don't have a clue about what those things should mean *to them*. Lord, give me a deep burden for those who need to hear about You, starting with the people in my own sphere of influence. Give me opportunities to share the best news of all time.

THINK ABOUT IT:

*Do you feel burdened for someone you know who needs
to hear the Gospel message? What will you do about it?*

THE GREATEST COMMANDMENT

Jesus said to him, " 'You shall love the LORD your God
with all your heart, with all your soul, and with all
your mind.' This is the first and great commandment."
MATTHEW 22:37–38 NKJV

Lord God, after all You've done for me, loving You should come easily to me. But it doesn't always. Sometimes I neglect You, and other times I feel distant. Thank You, Jesus, for speaking this first and great commandment, for it reminds me that a life in You starts with my commitment to love the One who is so committed to me. Father, help me to love You more and more deeply every day, starting with today. Show me ways to express my love to You.

THINK ABOUT IT:

What do you think loving God looks like
on a practical level? In what ways can
you express your love for God today?

SECURE IN JESUS

"And I give them eternal life, and they shall never perish; neither shall anyone snatch them out of My hand. My Father, who has given them to Me, is greater than all; and no one is able to snatch them out of My Father's hand."

JOHN 10:28–29 NKJV

Lord Jesus, I thank You for holding me securely in Your hand. Sometimes, I don't feel as secure as John 10 tells me I should. But I know that when I don't feel secure in You, it's most likely because *I've* drifted—I'm not abiding in You as I should. Draw me nearer to You, for that is where I feel secure, loved, and part of Your eternal family. Thank You for saving me and making me one of Your own.

THANK ABOUT IT:

Do you ever go through seasons when you don't feel secure in Jesus' love? What do you think causes that, and what can you do about it?

OVERCOMING DIFFICULTIES

"I've told you all this so that trusting me, you will be unshakable and assured, deeply at peace. In this godless world you will continue to experience difficulties. But take heart! I've conquered the world."

JOHN 16:33 MSG

Precious Jesus, I appreciate Your warning that I will have to endure difficulties. I've learned that trials are just part of living in a fallen world. But I thank You that You have promised me ultimate victory. I know that nothing will happen to me without Your approval, and I know that any suffering or trials I experience here on earth are part of Your ultimate plan. Lord, my difficulties look trivial when I compare them with what Your apostles endured. But I'm grateful that You care about them and that You've promised me ultimate victory.

--- **THINK ABOUT IT:** ---

What kinds of difficulties are you experiencing in this life today? Do you believe God truly cares about them and will give you victory?

STRENGTH AND COURAGE

*"Have I not commanded you? Be strong and
courageous! Do not be terrified nor dismayed,
for the LORD your God is with you wherever you go."*

JOSHUA 1:9 NASB

All-powerful God, I confess that I sometimes feel afraid. There have even been times when my fear all but paralyzed me. In Joshua 1:9, You told Your servant Joshua to be strong and courageous. But then You took that encouragement another huge step forward by telling Joshua he could be brave in the face of all potential dangers because You would always be with him. Lord, I believe that message is for me today too. When I feel afraid or anxious, remind me that You are and always will be with me. Help me to remember that You are bigger and mightier than any problem I'll ever face.

--- **THINK ABOUT IT:** ---

*Are you afraid or anxious about anything today? How do you
think God wants you to handle your fears and worries?*

YOUR REAL BATTLE

For our struggle is not against flesh and blood,
but against the rulers, against the authorities,
against the powers of this dark world and against
the spiritual forces of evil in the heavenly realms.
Ephesians 6:12 niv

All-powerful God, it's easy for me to think of people who stand against You and Your standards as my enemies. But You warn me that my true enemies are the devil and his spiritual minions, who will typically attack me where I'm weakest. Lord, I know that You tell me this as a warning so I can stand against the one who wishes me harm. I'm in a battle, Father, against an enemy I can't stand against on my own. But I know You are with me, and You have given me weapons not only to defend myself but to emerge victorious.

THINK ABOUT IT:

Who or what are the rulers, authorities, and powers of this
dark world? In what area do these forces attack you most?

SPIRITUAL DEFENSE SYSTEMS

Therefore put on the full armor of God, so that when the day of evil comes, you may be able to stand your ground, and after you have done everything, to stand. Stand firm then, with the belt of truth buckled around your waist, with the breastplate of righteousness in place, and with your feet fitted with the readiness that comes from the gospel of peace.

EPHESIANS 6:13–15 NIV

God of power and might, the Bible tells me that being a Christian on this side of eternity means going to war against spiritual forces. They work around the clock to keep people from knowing You and joining Your eternal kingdom. These same forces try to tempt me and other believers to sin—or at least to live a distracted life. But with the weapons of truth, righteousness, and readiness at my disposal, no spiritual enemy coming against me can succeed.

THINK ABOUT IT:

Why do you think the devil is so committed to attacking you on a spiritual level? How can you respond to those attacks?

A WEAPON OF OFFENSE

*In addition to all this, take up the shield of faith,
with which you can extinguish all the flaming arrows
of the evil one. Take the helmet of salvation and
the sword of the Spirit, which is the word of God.*

EPHESIANS 6:16–17 NIV

Lord Jesus, You've given me an overwhelming arsenal of weapons with which I can do spiritual battle. But one of those weapons is different from the others. The Bible calls itself "the sword of the Spirit," and it's the only one of those weapons that is offensive in nature. Remind me regularly that Your written Word is as powerful today as it was in Your days on earth, when You used it to repel the devil's temptations at the beginning of Your ministry.

——— THINK ABOUT IT: ———

*How can the Word of God help you as you
do spiritual battle here on earth? How can
you best arm yourself with this weapon?*

FOCUSING ON THE ETERNAL

We do not look at the things which are seen, but at the things which are not seen. For the things which are seen are temporary, but the things which are not seen are eternal.

2 CORINTHIANS 4:18 NKJV

Eternal God, Your written Word gives me many clues as to what waits for me in eternity. Some of what I can see in the natural realm, the things here on earth, are pleasant and wonderful to view. Others aren't so pleasant—there is a lot of ugliness in this world, and many people suffer because of it. But the beauty I can see here is nothing compared with what I'll witness in heaven. And the ugliness will be a distant memory once I'm in Your eternal kingdom. May I keep my focus on the eternal, not on what is here on earth.

THANK ABOUT IT:

What do you think eternal heaven will look like?
What kinds of things now on earth will not exist in heaven?

IN HIS TIMING

*"God is not a man, that He would lie, nor a son of man,
that He would change His mind; has He said, and will He
not do it? Or has He spoken, and will He not make it good?"*

NUMBERS 23:19 NASB

Trustworthy God, I've known people who I couldn't trust to keep their word. They may have made promises with the best of intentions, but they didn't always live up to their vows. It's never that way with You—never! You keep every one of Your promises and fulfill all Your purposes. I can trust You, even when Your timing differs from what I would want. But You are far wiser than I am, and I have to trust that You will fulfill Your promises when Your timing is right.

--- **THINK ABOUT IT:** ---

*Do you fully believe that God keeps all
His promises? Which of God's promises
are you waiting for Him to fulfill today?*

STAND UP, SPEAK UP

Speak up for those who cannot speak for themselves,
for the rights of all who are destitute.
PROVERBS 31:8 NIV

Compassionate God, I know there are any number of people groups who need someone to stand up and speak out on their behalf. I think of those who live in domestic and sexual slavery around the world. I think of the hungry, the homeless, and the infirmed who live in my own community. It's sad to consider what so many unfortunate people have to endure in today's world. But I know that You love them and value them as much as You love and value me. So help me to be a voice for those who can't speak up for themselves.

THINK ABOUT IT:

Have you ever asked God to show you
someone to speak up for? How can you
make your voice heard on behalf of others?

TRUSTING GOD WITH THE BAD STUFF

*And we know that God causes all things to
work together for good to those who love God,
to those who are called according to His purpose.*

ROMANS 8:28 NASB

Lord, You know that not everything that happens to me is good. Getting sick is not good. Neither is losing my job. And getting into a serious auto accident can throw a man's life into turmoil. But good can come out of any of those things—and many others—because I know You and am committed to following You through even the worst of circumstances. You've promised that You make all things work together for my good, making a positive out of things that are clearly negative. Please give me the faith and the peace to wait on You to do that.

THINK ABOUT IT:

When negative or difficult things happen in your life, how do you respond? Can you think of an example in your own life of God taking negatives and using them for your good?

HANDLING TEMPTATION

No temptation has overtaken you except such as is common to man; but God is faithful, who will not allow you to be tempted beyond what you are able, but with the temptation will also make the way of escape, that you may be able to bear it.

1 Corinthians 10:13 nkjv

Lord Jesus, I know that all men are tempted in one way or another. Satan tempted You at the start of Your earthly ministry, but You never sinned. I believe You beat temptation that day because You knew how to handle it. You relied on Your heavenly Father and on His Word. Lord, keep me humble—may I never believe that I have the ability to overcome temptation without Your help. Remind me to call out to You, and show me how I can best fight temptation.

THINK ABOUT IT:

What specific sins do you think the devil sees as your "weak spots"? How can you best overcome temptation?

DISCIPLINE: IT'S FOR YOUR OWN GOOD

My son, do not despise the LORD's discipline, and do not resent his rebuke, because the LORD disciplines those he loves, as a father the son he delights in.
PROVERBS 3:11–12 NIV

Loving Father, no one enjoys being disciplined, even when it's just a simple reprimand. I didn't enjoy it as a boy, and I don't enjoy it as a fully grown man. But You tell me that You discipline me out of Your love and delight for me. So discipline me, Lord. Reprove me when I need it, and help me to endure the reproof with the joy of knowing that it's for my own good. I probably won't enjoy it, but I welcome it—since it causes me to grow and mature in my faith, which in turn glorifies You.

THINK ABOUT IT:

What comes to mind when you hear the word discipline? In what ways do you think God disciplines those He loves?

SAVED TO SERVE

The righteous care about justice for the poor,
but the wicked have no such concern.
PROVERBS 29:7 NIV

Generous God, my heart breaks for those who don't have enough to live their lives—sufficient food, proper housing, enough money to pay for utilities. . .the list, sadly enough, goes on and on. Your Word teaches me that one evidence I have of Your Spirit living in me is my concern for the poor and mistreated. I've trusted You for salvation through Jesus Christ, and I am concerned. Now I ask You to motivate me and empower me to serve others. Lord, help me to be ever mindful of those in difficult life situations—and alert for opportunities to serve.

THINK ABOUT IT:

How important is it to God that you help the poor and
mistreated in this world? How can you find ways to serve
and help the less fortunate in your own community?

THE DANGER OF GREED

The greedy stir up conflict, but those
who trust in the LORD will prosper.
PROVERBS 28:25 NIV

Provider God, I know that You bless hard work, and I know that You want me to provide my family with the things they need in this life. You are not against financial prosperity, but You are against the sin of greed. You even warn that those who engage in greed put their eternal souls at peril. Your Word tells me to place my trust in You and Your promises of provision. When I truly do that, there is no place in my heart for greed. Lord, You are my Protector and Provider—I ask You to teach me to trust in You and not in my own striving for financial riches, lest I fall into the sin of greed.

THINK ABOUT IT:

What makes greed an especially dangerous sin?
How can you guard your heart against the sin of greed?

BEING A GIANT-SLAYER

*Then David said to the Philistine, "You come to
me with a sword, with a spear, and with a javelin.
But I come to you in the name of the LORD of hosts,
the God of the armies of Israel, whom you have defied."*

1 SAMUEL 17:45 NKJV

Mighty God, the young shepherd David needed Your help to slay a literal giant. I need Your help to slay some figurative giants. Sometimes I face life situations that are just too big for me to handle in my own strength. From where I stand, issues with my family, job, and ministry can look overwhelming. But I know that with You at my side, I can slay any of these giants. Thank You, Lord, that while I can't accomplish anything for You in my own strength, *with* You I can do anything!

THINK ABOUT IT:

*What kinds of "giants" are you facing today?
How can you defeat them?*

WHERE TO TURN WHEN TIMES ARE TOUGH

The LORD is good, a refuge in times of trouble.
He cares for those who trust in him.

NAHUM 1:7 NIV

Lord Jesus, when I first came to know You, I thought the rest of my life would be easy. It wasn't long, though, before I found out that walking with You presented its own difficulties. You didn't let me waver, and over time You've taught me the importance of turning to You when I face problems. Thank You for loving me and for always being my refuge. Help me to trust You for protection and empowerment when I'm going through rough times.

THINK ABOUT IT:

How do you usually respond when you face difficulties or obstacles in this life? Do you truly believe that God cares personally about your struggles?

SCRIPTURE INDEX